PUFFIN BOOKS

HOW YOU CAN
SAVE ᴛʜᴇ PLANET

HOW YOU CAN SAVE THE PLANET

HENDRIKUS VAN HENSBERGEN

FOREWORD BY ROBERT MACFARLANE, BESTSELLING AUTHOR OF *THE LOST WORDS*

PUFFIN

PUFFIN BOOKS

UK | USA | Canada | Ireland | Australia
India | New Zealand | South Africa

Puffin Books is part of the Penguin Random House group of companies
whose addresses can be found at global.penguinrandomhouse.com.

www.penguin.co.uk
www.puffin.co.uk
www.ladybird.co.uk

First published 2021

001

Text design by Anita Mangan

Printed in Great Britain by Clays Ltd, Elcograf S.p.A.

The authorized representative in the EEA is Penguin Random House
Ireland, Morrison Chambers, 32 Nassau Street, Dublin D02 YH68

A CIP catalogue record for this book is available from the British Library

ISBN: 978-0-241-45304-9

All correspondence to:
Puffin Books, Penguin Random House Children's
One Embassy Gardens, 8 Viaduct Gardens, London SW11 7BW

For Ludo

CONTENTS

FOREWORD

'The best arguments in the world won't change a person's mind,' says a character in *The Overstory*, Richard Powers's great recent novel about environmental activism. 'The only thing that can do that is a good story.' Well, I'm not sure I quite agree about arguments, but I do know that stories are some of the most world-shaping forces on Earth. And the book you hold in your hands is full of astonishing stories about remarkable people.

Take Lesein Mutunkei, for instance, who you will meet in a few pages' time. Lesein was himself inspired by the story of Wangari Maathai, who founded the Green Belt Movement, which has now planted more than 50 million trees in Kenya. Lesein began his own tree-planting campaign, Trees for Goals . . . and now here he is, inspiring others – including perhaps you – in turn to plant trees in their countries and landscapes. This is how change happens: from one tree, a global wildwood grows; from one person, a movement.

We all know that sometimes the environmental situation can feel overwhelming. Biodiversity is crashing. Temperatures and sea levels are rising. Sea ice is thinning, plastic pollution is growing. What can I do to change things? What's the point in even trying? The answer is that it's crucial to keep 'hope in the dark' alive, to borrow a phrase from the American writer Rebecca Solnit. That's what this book does brilliantly. It refuses to despair. Patiently, carefully, practically, beginning locally and scaling up to a planetary level, it shows how anyone can make a difference.

Hendrikus van Hensbergen knows more about transforming the world than most people. But he's far too modest to tell his own story. So let me do so briefly. When he was in his early twenties, Hendrikus decided that he wanted to do something to improve the health of the Earth. So he set out to found a charity called Action for Conservation, out of nothing other than the seed of an idea, his own determination, and his belief that young people needed to be given a voice when it came to saving the planet. That idea became a reality, and Action for Conservation is now one of the fastest-growing, most inclusive and most forward-looking environmental organizations in Britain. Its values are Wonder, Hope, Diversity, Action and Change – and you'll encounter some of the young people who've joined it in these pages, as well as all of those values.

So read on, and as you do so think of Lesein's message: 'Remember, you are never too small or too young to make an impact in the world. Know that everything you do counts. It is best to start now, because we don't have much time.'

ROBERT MACFARLANE, WRITER AND CAMPAIGNER

INTRODUCTION

This book is inspired by the amazing young people I have worked with at Action for Conservation in the UK and the many more that are leading change around the world. Here you will find step-by-step guides to things you can do to help save the planet and stories about young people, just like you, who are taking action. These change-makers and the actions they have taken are inventive, creative, fun and ambitious. Some are quiet and some are loud. But above all, they are hopeful.

Some actions in this book will work for you, some won't, and some could be changed to suit who you are and where in the world you live. Don't be afraid to experiment. Don't be afraid to fail and try again. You might want to follow each step carefully, or you might want to use them as an inspiration and a rough guide. Many of the organizations listed in the book are UK based, so if you live elsewhere, do look for organizations local to you if you need resources or advice. There are many more actions that aren't in this book, so don't stop here – start writing your own stories of hope and action.

This planet is our home, and it is dying. With over 60% of animal species in decline and one million animal and plant species at risk of extinction, we are running out of time to save the natural world. The United Nations is clear that we also have little time to limit global heating to 1.5°C and avoid the worst impacts of climate breakdown. It seems as though every day there are worse stories in the news. It can feel hopeless, especially when we know we need big changes at a global scale and those in power fail to take action. When faced with such a situation it is often easier for us to turn away. But more and more people are choosing not to. They are realizing that if we humans are the cause of these problems, then together we can also be the solution. People just like you and the young people you will meet in this book are finding ways to take action to turn things around and discovering a sense of hope in the process. It doesn't matter whether you start small or big – the important thing is that you take action. Together, we can save the planet.

Share your actions with us: #WeCanSaveThePlanet.

A NOTE ON ADULT SUPERVISION

Many things that are suggested in this book require adult supervision. Please be mindful of this and always check with an adult if you are not sure. For instance, if you are contacting people by phone, email or through social media, sending letters or posting content online, you should make a responsible adult aware, ask permission or get them to post on your behalf, and copy them in to any correspondence. If you are meeting with decision-makers or organizing events or projects out of school, then you will need to ensure an adult is with you or has given permission to you and any other young people involved. This is extremely important and is for your own safety. Before speaking to an adult about supervision, it is helpful to prepare detailed information about everything you plan to do so that they have a clear picture and can make an informed decision. See page 187 for other important tips and tricks to be aware of.

CHAPTER 1 NATURE

AMELIA'S STORY

'Small changes add up to make a big difference.'
AMELIA LAM

PHOTO © PUI FUN LAM

An albino squirrel, white from nose to tail, pricked its ears as it sat at the base of a tree in the middle of London. Its eyes were fixed on a young girl who stared straight back, holding its gaze. Amelia Lam's first encounter with this rare, otherworldly squirrel would stay with her as she grew up. It was a reminder that even in the middle of the city, nature can surprise you.

But it wasn't until she was fifteen that Amelia started to take action. She took part in an environmental competition at school. With some friends, she designed and made bird feeders out of old pencils. They hung the feeders outside and watched as birds they had never seen before visited their school in large numbers. Amelia's group won the competition. They spoke in an assembly about it, inspiring other students to act.

Then Amelia went on a guided kayak tour of the River Thames. She got to see her city from a completely different point of view. She had never thought about this deep, dark river, and all the life it holds, snaking its way through the heart of London, connecting borough after borough. The River Thames is home to fish, invertebrates, plants and even mammals, such as seals. But as she paddled, Amelia started noticing the amount of litter floating downstream, getting stuck along the banks and tangled in vegetation, litter that would be damaging for all of the life in the river.

Amelia decided to do something about it. She started by picking up litter every Sunday around Camberwell, where she lived, and she joined river clean-ups and collected rubbish in her kayak. Now that she feels connected to the river it has become her place to protect. For Amelia, the river is the city's mysterious watery heart, and she has become its guardian.

The more Amelia did to help nature, the more she wanted to do. She did a week of work experience with the Bat Conservation Trust (BCT), finding out about the only group of flying mammals on Earth. In many cultures bats are feared and misunderstood, resulting in a lack of protection. Amelia joined a bat survey, where she was able to watch them swoop over her head and listen to their calls on a bat detector. How could anyone fear these beautiful creatures, she wondered. She helped write and edit the charity's newsletter, and the whole experience inspired her to consider a future career in nature conservation.

Amelia felt motivated to shout louder about nature. She contributed to research that the government was doing on the future of the environment and she even featured in a film shown to their Science Advisory Council, a panel of the UK's leading scientists. She applied to join the London Wildlife Trust's Young People's Forum and was the youngest person ever to be selected. As part of the forum, she did some training in Media and Journalism, which has equipped her with the skills to be more effective in making her voice heard as an environmentalist. Now she is working hard to inspire other people to take action too.

AMELIA'S MESSAGE TO YOU

Everybody seems to use the planet for their own gain and one of the easiest ways we can give back is to look after it. I feel like the small changes I started to make at the beginning are now adding up. Small changes add up to make a big difference.

BUSY SKIES

JOIN AMELIA AND BUILD A RECYCLED BOTTLE BIRD FEEDER TO
ENCOURAGE OUR FLYING FRIENDS TO THRIVE

WHY?

- In the UK we have lost 40 million birds in 50 years.

- We are losing at least 40% of bird species globally due to
  harmful farming practices, the climate crisis, hunting and
  destruction of their habitats.

- Sadly, for many it is too late, and for some, like the turtle
  dove, where the numbers have dropped by 98% in the UK in
  the last 50 years, there is little hope left.

But we know what is causing these losses and we are working
hard to turn the situation around. Conservationists are
fighting for the future of our birds, and you can help them by
ensuring that those we do have survive.

WHAT YOU'LL NEED

A PENCIL OR AN OLD CHOPSTICK
(about one and a half times longer
than the width of your bottle)

SCISSORS

BIRD SEED
(or you can make your own
– see the next page)

A PLASTIC BOTTLE
WITH A LID

STRING

A NEWSPAPER OR MAGAZINE

STEP 1 – IDENTIFY YOUR SPOT

- You will need a tree branch, balcony or another fixed point to hang your bird feeder from. Make sure it is two metres off the ground so that the birds can feed safely out of reach of predators like cats.

- Choose a spot that is either closer than one metre to a window or more than four metres away from a window. This ensures that any birds visiting are either going to be flying too slowly to hurt themselves if they fly into a window or that they have enough room to avoid the window when they visit your feeder.

- Do a simple survey to identify which birds are present in your area before you get started (there are guides and apps on the Royal Society for the Protection of Birds [RSPB] and British Trust for Ornithology [BTO] websites).

STEP 2 – GATHER YOUR MATERIALS

- If you don't have an old plastic bottle to hand, do a litter pick! Always wear strong gloves when collecting litter and make sure to wash anything you find before using it.

- Think about what you are going to feed the birds. You can buy special bird seed mixes or make your own.

There are lots of recipes online for making your own bird seed mix. A simple option is to mix unsalted sunflower seeds, unsalted and chopped peanuts and raisins. Try to source organic ingredients; this means they have been grown in a way that isn't damaging to birds and other wildlife. You can also avoid plastic waste by trying to find a shop where you can buy loose ingredients.

STEP 3 – BUILD YOUR FEEDER

- First make sure your bottle is clean and dry.

- Stand the bottle upright and mark two holes opposite each other at least 3 cm up from the base of the bottle.

- Use your scissors or a barbecue skewer to create the holes and widen them to fit the pencil or chopstick. Make sure it fits snugly in the hole without falling out.

IMPORTANT

Make sure you are careful when cutting plastic and ask an adult to help if you are finding it difficult. Sharp plastic can hurt the birds so try to make the holes in the bottle as smooth as possible.

- Feed the pencil or stick through one hole and out the other side so that it sits level and the ends poke out of the bottle on either side (about a finger's length). This is where the birds will perch.

- Now carefully cut out a circular hole just above the pencil perch on either side. Keep it quite small, around 3 cm. This is for the birds to access the seed.

- To hang your feeder, pierce holes on opposite sides of the bottle just below the lid and feed string through. Create a loop by tying it together at the top.

- Make a cone out of a newspaper or magazine and use it to pour the seed mix into the top of the bottle so that it fills the bottle at least halfway up, making sure it is level with or covers the feeding hole.

- Mark the outside of the bottle with a pen to show how much bird seed you have put in and then monitor how much the birds have eaten.

- Now hang up your feeder and wait for the birds to arrive!

 TIP It is best not to put out whole peanuts in spring and summer as this can be a choking hazard for chicks.

STEP 4 – NEXT STEPS

- Make sure to keep replacing the seed as it gets eaten, particularly in winter, and wash the bottle out regularly to keep the feeder clean and the birds healthy.

- After you start to see some birds using your feeder, you can repeat your original survey to see which birds are visiting and whether there is a change.

- You can take part in the RSPB Big Garden Birdwatch and the BTO Garden Birdwatch, record what birds you see around your feeder and contribute important data to efforts to monitor the health of UK bird populations.

WHAT WILL IT ACHIEVE?

Survival is hard for birds; they need a lot of food to maintain a steady body temperature and enough energy to fly around. This is especially true for small birds and during the winter months. By providing extra food we will help more birds survive. If every person in the UK helped just one bird survive this coming winter, we would help over 66 million birds soar and sing into spring.

HOW TO BECOME A CITIZEN SCIENTIST

IDENTIFY AND RECORD THE WILDLIFE WHERE YOU LIVE

WHY?

- There have been five big mass species extinction events in the Earth's history. The most recent event included the extinction of the dinosaurs. Now, humans are causing the sixth.

- More than one million species of plants and animals are at risk of extinction across the world.

- We are losing hundreds of species a day, many of which have never been identified by scientists.

You can do something to save them. Take the first step by understanding what wildlife is around you.

STEP 1 – DECIDE ON YOUR AREA

WHAT IS A WILDLIFE SURVEY?

A wildlife survey is where you measure and record the species that exist in a specific area. This can include whether a species is present or not, how many individuals there are of each species and a range of other details.

- Pick the area you want to survey – this could be anywhere, such as your garden, your school grounds or a park.

- It might be useful to outline the area you pick using Google Maps or print out a map and do it by hand.

TIP If the area you pick is on land that belongs to someone else, make sure to ask for permission from the owner (see page 191 in the 'Tips and Tricks' chapter).

STEP 2 – PICK YOUR SURVEYS

The kind of survey you do depends on the habitats in your area. There are lots of free resources online that will help get you started. Don't feel you have to do everything. Here are just a few surveys you could try:

- For hedgerow plants, insects, tree health, earthworms, soil quality and air quality surveys look at the Open Air Laboratories (OPAL) Explore Nature website.

- For bird surveys look at the BTO website.

- The Woodland Trust has an ancient tree hunt.

- The charity Plantlife has wild flower survey guides for the city or the countryside.

- For amphibians and reptiles look at the charity Froglife's amphibian survey booklets or their Dragon Finder app.

- For bat surveys look at the BCT's National Bat Monitoring Programme.

- For other mammal surveys look at the People's Trust for Endangered Species (PTES) guide to spotting urban mammals, the National Biodiversity Network's page on mammal surveys or the Mammal Society's list of current mammal surveys.

- The UK Centre for Ecology and Hydrology have a UK Pollinator Monitoring Scheme for pollinating insects. Their website has information on how to carry out a 10-minute survey.

- For butterflies look at the Big Butterfly Count website.

- For earthworms you can also look at the Earthworm Watch website.

STEP 3 – PLAN YOUR SURVEYS

- You might want to ask a friend or family member to help you. Use the guides to plan out how you will conduct your surveys. Use the box below to take some notes.

- Design your surveys so that you can repeat them, and remember to keep them simple.

- Gather the materials you need to conduct your survey, print off any identification guides and prepare a table for recording your results.

STEP 4 – SURVEY, EAT, SLEEP, REPEAT

- Make sure you record your results accurately so that you know exactly what you have found. This is really vital information and many of the survey websites or apps will even offer you the chance to submit this data to help contribute to important scientific research and species monitoring!

- If you struggle to identify a species, take a photo so that you can identify it later on.

RECORDING YOUR DATA

You can either write down what you've found and where you've found it or you can use apps. Read the terms and conditions with a parent or guardian as some apps may require an adult to submit records or create an account on your behalf.

- You may want to repeat your observations over several days, or do day and night surveys to get the maximum amount of data.

- For plant and animal species try out the iRecord app or iNaturalist app.

- For trees try the Woodland Trust's Tree ID app.

- For birds look at the BTO BirdTrack app or eBird app.

STEP 5 – NEXT STEPS

- Use all the data you have collected to create a map of what you have found and where you have found it, as well as a guide to how you collected it. You can include drawings or photos of some of the species you have found too. Share this with others over the internet by writing a blog (see Action 24 on page 135).

WHAT WILL IT ACHIEVE?

Through many of the surveys listed, you can contribute real data to scientific research projects and become a 'citizen scientist'. The work of citizen scientists is very important in building up a picture of changes in wildlife across the world. By surveying wildlife, you will also create a firm foundation for your other actions and be able to measure what positive changes you have made in your local area.

FUN IN THE FIELD

ORGANIZE A FIELD TRIP FOR FRIENDS
OR STUDENTS AT YOUR SCHOOL

WHY?

*   Field trips have been in decline for some time and so fewer
    and fewer young people get an opportunity to experience
    and learn about wildlife outdoors while at school.
*   It doesn't matter whether the trip is far from home or a
    visit to a local nature reserve – learning outside has been
    proven to provide huge benefits. It enables us to understand
    nature better and feel more connected to it and has benefits
    for our mental and physical health and well-being.

Take matters into your own hands and help organize a trip.

STEP 1 – RESEARCH THE BENEFITS

*   Do some research on the benefits of outdoor education
    (there are a lot of benefits!), so that you can make a
    powerful case to your teachers.
*   Break down the evidence into categories, such as:
    *   Education and learning
    *   Mental and physical health
    *   Skills development.

STEP 2 – IDENTIFY A LOCATION

*   Look around for a possible location. Start with a green
    space close to your school or search online for field study
    centres, such as those run by the Field Studies Council
    (FSC), and local nature reserves run by, for example, the
    Wildlife Trusts or the RSPB.
*   Research whether they already host school groups or have
    facilities that could accommodate a group.

- Contact any likely places to find out more and explain your ideas.
- Shortlist possible locations, some nearby and others further away, and write down a list of bullet points on what they can provide.

STEP 3 – GET PERMISSION

- Create a plan that includes your research from Steps 1 and 2 and then approach a teacher you think might be interested in the idea and present it to them, explaining why you would like to organize a field trip. If you can, tie your trip in with a subject, such as Biology or Geography.
- Offer to help recruit other students, create a budget for costs, such as transport and accommodation, and offer to fundraise if needed.
- If the first teacher you approach isn't supportive of the idea, then you can always ask others until you find one who says yes.

STEP 4 – PLAN THE TRIP

- Agree which location to visit with the teacher. The first trip could be nearby and act as a test run for somewhere further away that involves overnight stays.
- Decide on the focus of the trip and get in touch with whoever will be leading the activities at the site to plan what you will be doing.
- Pick a date that will work for the school and students.
- Get students to sign up to the trip. If there is going to be lots of interest and limited places you could run a competition to pick who attends or agree to organize more than one trip so that everyone can benefit from the experience.
- List key items for everyone to bring, including suitable outdoor clothing, food and drink, and any field equipment required.

- Put someone in charge of taking photos or vlogging on the day to document the experience, but remember to get permission first.

STEP 5 – NEXT STEPS

- Do a feedback survey after the trip to get students' opinions.
- Write a blog or an article for your school newsletter using eye-catching photos or videos or give an assembly on the experience and show your vlogs to inspire other students to apply for or organize the next trip!
- Use positive feedback you received and the confidence the teacher and school now have in you to plan a follow-up trip to the same site or another location.

WHAT WILL IT ACHIEVE?

The benefits of outdoor education and time spent in nature are clear and significant. By taking the initiative and organizing a trip like this you could change the culture at your school and encourage more learning outside the classroom. You will also forge links between your school and conservation organizations and field centres that could be long-lasting and have the potential to give many more young people life-changing experiences in the future.

LESEIN'S STORY

'Know that everything you do counts.'

LESEIN MUTUNKEI

Lesein Mutunkei picked up the last handful of earth. He felt the soil crumble between his fingers as he dropped it in the hole. It was satisfying to see the earth piling up around the roots of the small tree. Once he had finished planting, he watered his tree carefully. Lesein was seven years old. He grew up in the city of Nairobi in Kenya. His family liked to go camping in the nearby countryside and occasionally they would plant a tree. Over the next few years Lesein heard more about deforestation and climate breakdown in the news. He was shocked to find out that Kenya was losing 50,000 hectares of forest each year, the equivalent of 164 football pitches every day. He realized that planting trees is a natural solution to the climate crisis as they absorb carbon dioxide in the air as they grow.

At the age of 12, Lesein came up with a simple idea. He loved football and so for every goal he scored, he would plant a tree. He called this initiative Trees for Goals. Knowing that he was going to do something good for the planet if he scored a goal motivated him to play better. Students at his school started to ask what he was doing and so Lesein decided to get other students involved to make a bigger impact. The school was planning a trip to Amboseli National Park in southern Kenya. Lesein spoke to his teachers about planting trees while they were there, and the school agreed.

When he got back home, Lesein thought about how he could make his simple idea more effective. What if, for every goal scored, 11 trees were planted, one to represent each player on the team? After all, every goal is a collaborative team effort. The idea stuck. The school started Trees for Goals in their football, rugby and basketball teams and his football club adopted his idea. Soon they had planted nearly a thousand trees around Nairobi.

Lesein decided he wanted to expand his approach across Kenya, but he would need some help. Fortunately, the Ministry of Environment and Forestry noticed his campaign on social media. He was invited to meet their board and the minister. They discussed how his approach could engage young people in the environment and agreed to provide him with trees.

Lesein began to get more and more media attention for his simple, clever idea. His school was so impressed that it nominated him to join the very first United Nations (UN) Youth Climate Summit in New York. He boarded the plane for his first trip outside Kenya. New York felt so big, with such high buildings. At 15 years old, he was one of the youngest at the conference, and he felt so inspired by all the other young people he met. When he returned, he was invited to meet Kenya's President and plant a tree with him.

Lesein dreams of creating a forest of Trees for Goals in each county of Kenya, then a forest of Trees for Goals in each country in Africa. He wants FIFA to adopt his approach and famous football players to start planting trees. Lesein believes we need to keep solutions simple and that sport can educate people and inspire them to do more for our precious environment.

LESEIN'S MESSAGE TO YOU

One of my inspirations is Wangari Maathai. She founded the Green Belt Movement, which has planted 51 million trees in Kenya. She said that it is the little things we do that will make the difference. My little thing is Trees for Goals. Remember you are never too small or too young to make an impact in the world. Know that everything you do counts. It is best to start now, because we don't have much time.

THE ORIGINAL SKYSCRAPERS

JOIN LESEIN AND FIND THE BEST PLACE TO PLANT TREES SO THAT THEY CAN CLEAN UP OUR AIR AND PROVIDE HOMES FOR WILDLIFE

TREES ARE AWESOME AND LIFE-GIVING. THEY:

- trap pollutants and absorb carbon dioxide as they grow and release the oxygen that keeps us alive.
- provide homes for wildlife – a single adult oak tree can have hundreds of different species living in and on it!
- prevent flooding and cool our cities.
- make us feel better – they are proven to be good for our mental health.

WHY?

- Globally, an area of forest as big as the UK is lost every year as trees are cut down or burnt, mainly to provide space for farming.
- We are losing irreplaceable forests and the unique animals and plants that live in them.
- But there is hope, both in the city and the countryside. For example, City of Trees aims to plant three million trees in Greater Manchester, one for every resident. Trees already cover 20.6% of the city, compared to 13% across the UK as a whole.

There is so much more space for trees wherever we live and a number of different organizations are working hard to create more forest and woodland. Join the movement by planting your very own tree.

WHAT YOU'LL NEED

A WOODEN STAKE
OR BAMBOO CANE
to support the tree as it grows

A SPADE

YOUR SAPLING
(a young tree)

A TREE GUARD
to protect your sapling as it
grows (optional)

STEP 1 – PICK A PLACE TO PLANT

IMPORTANT

Check if you need permission to plant a tree in the area you've picked (see page 191 in the 'Tips and Tricks' chapter).

- Make sure there is enough space for the tree to grow.
- Avoid places with overhead power lines or where a tree might block a driver's view at a junction.
- Be mindful of nearby buildings or areas with paving stones, decking or tarmac as they may interfere with root growth.

 Have a look at the Woodland Trust's helpful planting planning tool and other guidance documents before you start to make sure planting a tree is appropriate.

- Trees need soil that isn't compacted (squashed together) to allow air and water to flow around the roots, helping the tree grow.

SIGNS OF COMPACTED SOIL INCLUDE:

- Water forming in pools or running off the surface.
- Bare areas where weeds and grass aren't growing.
- Areas too hard to dig.

STEP 2 – PICK YOUR TREE AND PLAN

- Decide what type of tree you'd like to plant. You can look online to see what would work best for the area you've chosen (see page 205 for a list of useful resources).

 Pick trees that are native to the country where you are planting them, as they are better for wildlife and adapted to local conditions.

This is your most important decision. You are planting hope and seeding wonder. You are creating a legacy long after you are gone. Choose wisely . . .

- Think about changes that could affect your tree in the future like changes in temperature, rainfall, or how the land might be used. Make sure that the tree you choose stands a good chance of weathering these changes.
- Plan when you are going to plant. In the UK, the Royal Horticultural Society (RHS) recommends planting between the colder months of October and April.

STEP 3 – FIND YOUR TREE

- You might be able to get your tree for free. If you want to plant more than one tree and you are organizing this with your school or a community group, then you can get free trees for planting from the Woodland Trust.
- You can even set up your own group and get their tree packs too.
- Make sure you look out for free tree giveaways on the internet; organizations often give trees away for planting, particularly in urban areas.
- If you can't source any for free, you can buy trees from the Woodland Trust for less than £7.

STEP 4 – PLANT FOR THE FUTURE

- Here comes the exciting part! Dig a hole that is a little bigger and deeper than the size of your tree roots.

- Chop up and loosen the soil with the edge of your spade and mix in any grass with the soil at the bottom of the hole.

- Check the depth by placing your tree in the hole and ensuring that the collar (the point just above the roots where the tree was previously growing above ground) is level with the top of the hole. It is important that the hole isn't too shallow or too deep. If it is the wrong depth add or remove soil until it is right.

- Place the tree in an upright position and fill in the hole. Make sure that you press the soil in around the trunk and roots, but not so hard that it becomes compacted. Use a strong bamboo cane to provide support for the tree by pushing it firmly into the soil next to the trunk and tying them to each other. You can also use a tree guard or tree spiral to protect your growing tree from animals that might eat it, like deer. Look for more environmentally friendly options that are biodegradable.

- Once your tree is planted, water it immediately and then again after about 2–3 weeks or follow the instructions that came with it.

- Make sure to weed the area around your tree for a couple of years after planting it as it becomes established and takes root. Avoid using harmful chemicals to get rid of weeds.

- If you are using a tree guard, remember to check that this is firmly pressed into the ground.

CELEBRATE!

During or after planting your tree, hold an event to mark this special moment. Bring everyone together to celebrate your achievement and talk about why you are doing this, explain your plans to plant more trees and encourage others to join you.

WHAT WILL IT ACHIEVE?

One tree is as effective at reducing temperatures as 10 large air conditioning units working 20 hours a day. It can produce enough oxygen for four people and will have removed up to one tonne of carbon dioxide by the time it is 40 years old. Imagine how much good your tree will do over its whole lifetime. Can there be a better legacy than that?

ESTHER'S STORY

'If we don't act, today's young people will have to explain why to future generations.'

ESTHER BIRD

PHOTO © CHARISSE KENION

Esther Bird carefully typed her name into the box. As she clicked submit and then refreshed the page to see the number of signatures on her own petition go up by one, she felt a buzz of excitement. The petition was about banning single-use plastics at her school.

Esther grew up in Macclesfield. She had always felt strongly about environmental issues and at the age of 11 she had decided to take action. It was easy to create a petition and share it online, and within three months she had hundreds of signatures. At school, she gave an assembly about her petition, and after hearing Esther talk, the head teacher decided to help her set up a meeting with the school's catering company.

At first the company agreed to ban single-use plastics by the end of the year, but after lots of delays, it became clear Esther would have to negotiate a compromise with the company to make change happen. The company agreed to a new approach, phasing out plastic bit by bit. This wasn't what Esther had hoped for, but she realized it could work well. It gave time for alternatives to be found and for students to adapt. First, plastic bottles were replaced by cans. Then, plastic wrappers for cakes were replaced by trays and cardboard boxes. Now, almost all plastics have been banned.

After the success of the single-use plastic ban, Esther decided to set up an inter-school eco group to meet students from lots of different schools and share ideas. With the help of a local community group and the town's mayor she invited students from five secondary schools to a meeting at the town hall. Her new 'Eco-Youth' group started to grow, and soon primary school children joined in too.

In the first Eco-Youth meeting, Esther shared some photos of eco-bricks: single-use plastic bottles stuffed so full of plastic rubbish they are hard and heavy enough to be used as bricks. She thought they were a great way to get rid of plastic waste and build something new. She had an idea to use them to create beds for wild flower meadows. She spotted an opportunity to apply for funding from Kew Gardens and decided to make an application. A few weeks later an email appeared in her inbox. She had been successful. Kew had awarded her £500 to pursue the project. She shared the news with the group and they got to work planning the project.

They researched wild flowers and bought the right seeds to help pollinating insects, such as bees. Esther's teacher offered to grow the wild flowers in pots in her back garden. The same community group who had helped Esther find a space to meet put the word out on social media – people across Macclesfield started making eco-bricks. A local cafe got in touch and offered to store all the bricks until they needed them. A local church offered them space to build the beds. Success! Then the group came up with the clever idea to engage more people by building the beds and planting the flowers with the community during a forthcoming festival. The festival organizers agreed and said they could have a stall. It was all going so smoothly – almost too good to be true.

Four weeks before the festival they found out they would have to get planning permission for the beds from the council. They were stuck. This seemed too big a problem to overcome. But they weren't defeated yet. They decided to adapt their plans, build the beds as temporary structures for the festival, and move them afterwards. The festival was a huge success, and afterwards they decided they would give the beds a permanent home at each of the schools involved.

Esther hasn't stopped there. She has spoken at events, given a TEDx talk, become an Ambassador for the #IWill campaign for youth social action, helped launch the 2019 State of Nature report (which contains information about the decline of British wildlife, and how we can turn the situation around) and been tree planting with the Woodland Trust. She even set up a youth strike for climate in Macclesfield. The group numbers have grown from five to 200 people, and now Esther is focusing on making the strikes more accessible to everyone, like people who can't afford it or have access needs. And it all started with a simple petition.

ESTHER'S MESSAGE TO YOU

Children travelling to and from school in a city 'smoke' the equivalent of a box of cigarettes a day because of air pollution. If we don't act, today's young people will have to explain why to future generations. Even if it is not for the planet, it is about us too. It will directly impact us in the future. Even if you don't care about animals, you can do something for yourself and your friends. Even if it is small. Some people think we should just leave it to adults and that we are too young to worry about it. But in 11 years climate breakdown will be irreversible and I will still be classed as a youth activist. We'll still be young when it becomes catastrophic so we need to act while we can still change the outcome!

ACTION 5 PLANT FOR POLLINATORS

BUILD AND PLANT A VERTICAL WILD FLOWER MEADOW TO HELP POLLINATING INSECTS

INSECTS ARE VITAL TO LIFE ON EARTH. THEY:

- develop healthy soils.
- are food for all sorts of other animals and plants.
- break down waste.
- pollinate plants (many of which provide us with food).

WHY?

- Around the world, over 40% of insect species are declining and at risk of extinction.
- Wild flower meadows are an important home for many pollinating insects.
- Just one square metre (an area measuring one metre by one metre in size) of wild flower meadow can support up to 40 different species.

The good news is that we can all create space for wild flowers to help insects thrive. Like Esther, if we think a little differently, we can all find one square metre.

WHAT YOU'LL NEED

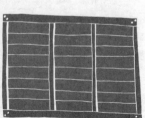

LARGE PLASTIC BOTTLE

A BRICK WALL OR A SOLID FENCE

 SOIL

 NATIVE WILD FLOWER SEEDS

WOODEN BATTENS
(long, thin pieces of wood that can be screwed to a wall or fence)

PEAT-FREE COMPOST

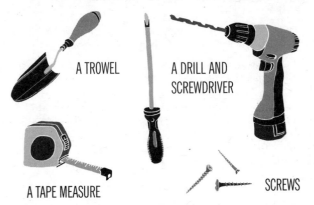

A TROWEL

A DRILL AND SCREWDRIVER

A TAPE MEASURE

SCREWS

STEP 1 – IDENTIFY YOUR SPOT

- Pick an outside wall or fence that insects (and you) can access. It doesn't have to be close to other green spaces. Look for a sunny spot where you will be able to water the plants easily.

- If you'd like to inspire others with your meadow, find a place that is visible, like near the entrance to a building.

IMPORTANT

If the wall or fence belongs to someone else, you'll need to get permission to use it (see page 191 in the 'Tips and Tricks' chapter).

STEP 2 – DESIGN YOUR WALL AND GATHER YOUR MATERIALS

- Use a tape measure to work out how big your vertical meadow will be.

- Start with a small area (like a square metre). You can always make the meadow bigger over time.

- Think about your structure. Do you want a wooden frame that attaches to the wall or fence, or one that leans against it?

- Research how far apart the rows should be and make sure there will be enough space on the wooden frame for all your containers.

- For the frame you will need wooden battens (see page 188 in the 'Tips and Tricks' chapter). You'll need at least four pieces for the outside structure and 3–4 pieces to create rows for your containers. You can easily adapt and increase this as you go along.

- Do a litter pick and collect large plastic bottles to turn into plant containers.

TIP

To convert a bottle into a plant container, remove the label, wash the bottle and then cut it in half. Make a few holes in the base to help water drain out and you have made yourself a free, recycled water-bottle plant pot. Don't forget to recycle any plastic you don't use!

- Mix normal garden soil with a little low-nutrient peat-free compost – go to your local garden centre for this or speak to your school about getting hold of some. A lot of UK wild flowers actually like soil that is quite low in nutrients, so don't add too much compost.

WHY WE USE PEAT-FREE COMPOST

Peat is a type of soil that develops in boggy environments. It provides a home for wildlife and stores huge amounts of carbon. The peat in shops has been dug up from a peat bog, so when you use peat-free compost you are ensuring that these important environments are not destroyed.

- Choose your seeds. It is important to have a mixture of native plants – do some research and create a list of 5–10 species (see page 189 in the 'Tips and Tricks' chapter and page 206 in the list of useful resources).
- Check the planting instructions for your seeds. Autumn is often the best time for planting.

STEP 3 – BUILDING YOUR STRUCTURE

- Now that you have everything ready, it shouldn't take too long to create your vertical meadow.

IMPORTANT
Ask an adult for help with the next step.

- Screw four battens together into a square frame. Create rows by screwing battens across the frame. To make the frame stronger you can then screw pieces running in the opposite direction to make a chequerboard structure (see diagram).

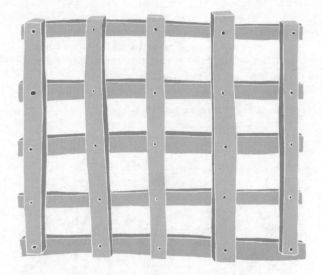

- Now attach this structure to the wall or fence with screws using the drill. Make sure to attach the structure very firmly in six to eight places.

- Using two or more screws, attach your recycled pots. Place these anywhere on the wooden frame you have created, but space them out at regular intervals, making sure there are gaps between them. Attach them near the top of the pots, so that they hang down below the batten.

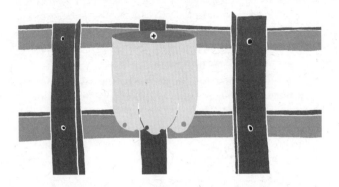

Test out the first pot by filling it with plenty of wet soil and compost mixture to make sure that it can take the weight. If it can't, then you may need to adapt your design by placing a small piece of wood inside the pot, which you screw through, or by creating a wire basket for each pot. (Look at the end of this action to see how you can do this.)

- This is also a good time to assess the number of pots and reduce them if you feel there won't be enough space for the plants to grow.

STEP 4 – PLANTING YOUR MEADOW

- Fill the pots with your soil and compost mixture.
- Plant your seeds and water them, following the planting instructions on the seed packet.
- As your plants grow, sit back and watch insects make a home and forage for food in your vertical meadow!

OTHER WAYS YOU CAN MAKE YOUR MEADOW

1. Fix your pots along the top of a fence, place them on a windowsill or use an old bucket as a container instead. (Don't forget to create drainage holes and fill it to the top with soil so that your wild flowers get enough light.) You'll need fewer materials and you can create a smaller meadow more quickly.

2. Create a leaning structure by just using a flat piece of wood instead of wooden battens.

3. If you can't find any large plastic bottles, ask around your community or source some old plant pots from a garden centre or school.

4. Instead of screwing the pots directly to your structure, create a wire basket by running wire in a cross beneath the pot and then around the pot and hooking this to a nail or screw in the frame.

WHAT WILL IT ACHIEVE?

In the UK we have lost almost all of our meadows – they now cover just 1% of the country. If everyone in the UK made a one metre square vertical meadow it would create enough wild flower meadow to cover over 9,000 football pitches and provide vital space for thousands of species.

REWILD YOUR GREEN SPACE

MAKE A PRETTY PARK MORE WILD!

- -

WHY?

- All around the world wild habitats where species live are being lost to expanding farmland, new buildings and roads.
- Habitat loss is the biggest cause of wildlife declines, particularly for species that are at risk of extinction.

All is not lost. We can farm in a more nature-friendly way and create more space for wildlife. Towns and cities full of parks and gardens can become homes for wildlife. If we learn to be less neat and more imaginative, we can create a wilder, more hopeful future that sees life thriving in and among our homes.

STEP 1 – IDENTIFY A PARK OR GREEN SPACE THAT COULD BE MORE WILD

- Look around where you live: is there any green area that's a little bit . . . boring? Perhaps it's just all uniform, flat grass and the odd tree?
- If you had complete freedom, how would you change this place? What is it missing? Is it wild flowers, trees or bees? Draw some pictures, make notes or use a computer game or program to visualize your ideas. These ideas will come in useful later.

STEP 2 – BUILD A TEAM AND MAKE A PLAN

- Speak to your friends or your school eco-team about your plan and explain the opportunity to create positive change by making your chosen area wilder.

TIP If your school doesn't have an eco-team, this project could be a good excuse to set one up (have a look at Action 21 on page 125 and page 193 in the 'Tips and Tricks' chapter).

- Suggest forming a group to carry out your project – the more people you involve the better. You may want to give people different roles, like planning, researching, getting permissions or sourcing materials.

- Do a survey of your chosen project site and see what wildlife is already there (use Action 2 on page 8 to do this). Make sure you ask for permission (see page 191 in the 'Tips and Tricks' chapter)!

- Draw a plan of the area as it is now, including any features or species you've found.

- With your group, draw another plan of what you would like the site to look like.

TIP Use your ideas from Step 1 and other actions in Chapter 1 for inspiration and to help you design specific features. Could it be planting wild flowers like Esther or trees like Lesein?

- Discuss what materials you will need to create these changes and what additional support you might need.

- What changes are the biggest priority for wildlife? If it helps, you can break this list down into three categories, those features that are essential for wildlife, those that you would love to have but that might not all be possible, and then a few dream ideas that are bigger and more radical!

STEP 3 – GET PERMISSION AND FINALIZE YOUR PLANS

- Next, turn your plan, with all the features you discussed, into a bullet point list and ask the landowner for permission (see page 191 in the 'Tips and Tricks' chapter).

- Always be ambitious with what you ask for. That way you are in a better position to negotiate. Be prepared to change your plans at this stage.

- Agree a final set of actions with the landowner, adapting your plans as necessary.

- Think about how much time each feature will take and when you will set aside time to work on them and in what order they will work best.

- Work out a budget. The cost of your project will depend on how big it is, how challenging it is and whether or not you can find materials and tools for free. You can find guides to sourcing materials, creating a budget and fundraising for your project in the 'Tips and Tricks' chapter.

- Think about how you will make your project a safe space for all those involved. Do you need an adult's assistance? If yes, then who are they and when are they available to help you?

STEP 4 – GO WILD AND TAKE ACTION

- Start delivering your inspiring and ambitious plans. Some things won't happen the way you planned or might not happen at all. Be determined, be adaptable and don't give up. Exciting and unexpected outcomes will happen too.

- As some of your ideas become reality and your features begin to take shape, other people are likely to become interested. Make sure you stop to explain what you are doing to people who show an interest and encourage them to help out. You could even set up a volunteer programme (see page 200 in the 'Tips and Tricks' chapter).

CELEBRATE!

When you complete each feature, hold an event to mark this special moment. Bring everyone together to celebrate your achievement and talk about why you are doing this, explain your plans for the other features and encourage others to join you.

- After six months to a year, repeat the survey you carried out in Step 2 and see what new species are finding a home in your site. You can do this again after a longer period and see even greater changes.

STEP 5 – NEXT STEPS

- Spread the word by creating a website, vlogs, a film or an information board in a wild place!
- Look at Action 9 on page 51 to turn your wild green space into one part of a network of connected areas for wildlife.
- Look at Action 30 on page 172 to ensure that you end the use of harmful chemicals.

WHAT WILL IT ACHIEVE?

If you can create new ecosystems and homes for plants and animals in a green space, then you will help bring new life into the world. Your hard work will act as a dramatic, positive statement to your community and your vision and passion will give rise to ideas and inspiration, growing like green shoots in others.

KABIR'S STORY

'Get out there and explore and save nature on your doorstep.'

KABIR KAUL

PHOTO © KATE PETERS

Kabir Kaul could tell what it was before he opened it. He picked up the present and turned it around in his hands, feeling the texture of the wrapping paper. The weight felt about right, so did the size – a pair of binoculars. At just eight years old, Kabir was already interested in the pigeons that cruised past his window and the blackbirds that hopped on his doorstep. He often imagined what else might be out there and now he could explore even further. He didn't know it at the time, but these binoculars would be the key to a whole new world.

Over the next few years Kabir used his binoculars to spot and identify birds all over London and around the UK. He became incredibly knowledgeable and, at the age of 12, he wrote a letter to the RSPB about how these birds' homes were disappearing. The RSPB's youth magazine, *Wingbeat*, got in touch and asked Kabir to write an article for them.

He really enjoyed it. He felt it was a way he could share his voice and convince others to help save birds. A year later, he created a blog where he could write exactly what he wanted and joined social media to learn more about the problems facing his local area. He discovered all sorts of organizations working to protect wildlife and inspire young people. Before, he had felt alone in caring about these problems; now there was a community of other young people who wanted to make a difference.

While searching online for places to visit and look for wildlife where he lived, Kabir realized that there was no map of all the wildlife areas across London. He was surprised. How could there not be a guide? Surely this would help people visit these areas and become more interested in wildlife. So he decided to do something about it. On his blog he started to put together a map of wildlife sites. He learnt about all the different types of protection given to these areas by local councils, the UK government and the European Union. There were Sites of Special Scientific Interest, Local Nature Reserves, Special Protection Areas, and so many more! The number of areas on his map grew and grew. He began to feel like a bird soaring over the city looking down. He decided to go and visit as many of the sites as possible. He then uploaded his walking routes to the map, so that other people could follow in his footsteps.

People started to come across the map on social media. They visited his blog and talked about it. London is one of the greenest cities in the world – 47% of it is classified as green space – but few people are aware of this. Kabir's map was inspiring people to get out and experience what he calls the 'wild side of London', the patchwork of green and blue among the grey.

Organizations started asking him to give talks and become an ambassador for their work. He even had a new birdwatching hide named after him in a nature reserve. He started conducting surveys at Broadwater Lake Nature Reserve in the Colne Valley – an important site for migratory birds that is threatened by plans for a new railway line.

The threats facing this site and others have motivated Kabir to take a stand for wildlife. He is working closely with the team at London National Park City to inspire people to think about the city differently, to see beyond the tarmac and traffic and form a new relationship with the wildlife living among them. He wants to turn his map into an app so that more people can use it.

Kabir was recently recognized for all his hard work. The BTO selected him for its prestigious Marsh Award, he was named as one of the *Big Issue*'s Top 100 Changemakers of 2020 and the Prime Minister recognized him with a Points of Light award. What makes Kabir happiest, though, is when people approach him and say, 'I have grown up here and your map has shown me a nature site right on my doorstep that I had never noticed.' That is when he knows he is making a difference.

KABIR'S MESSAGE TO YOU

Get involved with local organizations and volunteer groups and help rewild and restore green and blue space locally. If you have a balcony or garden you can create a pond, wildlife habitat or nest boxes. All these small changes together will help biodiversity. It will boost your well-being. Get out there and explore and save nature on your doorstep.

ACTION 7 WALK ON THE WILD SIDE

PLAN AND LEAD A WILDLIFE EDUCATION WALK IN YOUR SCHOOL OR A LOCAL PARK

- -

WHY?

- Leading a wildlife walk for your family or friends is a great way for you to learn about wildlife and encourage others to take an interest and start on a path to taking action to protect the planet.

- Getting out and appreciating nature benefits our mental and physical health. Learning about nature locally and how to identify different species creates a deeper connection to your area and everything that lives in it.

You can host a wildlife walk anywhere – it doesn't matter if you are in a city or the middle of the countryside. For example, over 14,000 species of plants, animals and fungi have been recorded in London, and Sites of Importance for Nature Conservation cover almost 20% of the city. These official sites are just the tip of the iceberg; many more sites and walks have been recorded and mapped by London National Park City and by Kabir Kaul on his *Kaul of the Wild* blog.

STEP 1 – FIND A ROUTE

- Find a walking route that will take in a variety of interesting habitats or species. This could be through your school grounds, a local park or in a larger nature reserve.

- Start with a mini-route – you can always build up to longer routes. Aim for a route that takes 15 minutes to walk. Once you factor in stops and short talks your walk could be 30–40 minutes long in total.

STEP 2 – PLAN THEN PRACTISE, PRACTISE, PRACTISE

- Buy, download or borrow some animal and plant identification guides or apps and start walking your route and identifying what species are there.

- Make notes on what you have found and then see how often these species are present each time you walk your route.

 Use Action 2 on page 8 for examples of simple species identification and monitoring.

- Walk your route enough times to identify species and decide where you will stop and talk about interesting wildlife.

- Plan how you will start your walk. You will want a short introduction to what you will be seeing.

- Plan four three-minute scripts to talk about four different species that will definitely be present during your walk and decide where you will stop to talk about them. This will probably be plants or fungi that can't move, although if there are signs of an animal species that you know for certain will be there, like holes made by an animal, then you could make that a focus.

- Decide how to get your audience involved! Start each script by asking them to look around to see if they can spot the species. Then, before you explain what it is and give some facts about why it is important, tell them that there will be a quiz at the end. That way, you will ensure that they are really listening to you! If you can find rarer species or those of particular interest to conservationists this might make your talk even better.

- Plan a further five three-minute scripts for other animals, like birds or insects, that you have seen on most of your walks, but not all. This will give you something to say if you do see them when you are leading your walk. Warn your audience that there's a chance they might not be there on the day of your walk – this will build excitement if you do see them, or help with the disappointment if you don't.

- Encourage everyone to ask questions during the walk and to engage in conversation with you and each other. It will be even more fun that way.

- Plan a short quiz as a way to end your walk.

- Do a practice run of the full walk and all your scripts with a trusted friend or family member and get their feedback.

STEP 3 – FIND YOUR AUDIENCE

- Make any final changes to your walk and script then decide on a date and time for your first walk and how many people you will take. Make sure you leave yourself about 30 minutes of time before the walk actually starts to accommodate latecomers.

- Advertise among your friends.

- You can always start with friends who are already interested in nature as a way to practise your walk further and then explore ways to convince those who are less engaged to join you and learn about their local area.

STEP 4 – WALK ON THE WILD SIDE

- Once you have enough people signed up for your first walk, make sure to let them know in advance if they need to bring any equipment or particular clothing.

- Enjoy the walk. You might find that a few people drop out on the day or that the walk doesn't go exactly as planned – things rarely run perfectly. Stay motivated! What is important is that you learn and continue to improve.

- Do gather feedback from people who attend. This is the only way you will learn what you could improve on and also find out what is working really well!

STEP 5 – NEXT STEPS

- Learn some new routes and some new species after you have done your first walk a few times.
- Vlog during your walks or write short guides to your walking routes, explaining which paths to take. Include information on the species people can expect to find. Use pictures and photos to make these interesting and then publish them on a blog or website using Action 24 on page 135 for guidance.

WHAT WILL IT ACHIEVE?

People walk through wildlife areas right on their doorstep without ever truly looking at what is there and appreciating the value these places hold for wildlife. Sometimes it just takes someone to gently open their eyes to what is right there in front of them. You can be that person – you can dramatically change the way people look at their communities and see nature as a part of them.

HIGHWAYS FOR HEDGEHOGS

CREATE HOLES FOR HEDGEHOGS AND OTHER SMALL
CREATURES TO MOVE FROM ONE GREEN SPACE TO ANOTHER

WHY?

- Over half of all known mammal species globally are decreasing in numbers.

- In the UK's rural areas, hedgehog numbers have fallen by more than half since 2000 partly due to a decline in insect numbers (their main food), loss of their habitat, including hedgerows, and the use of poisonous slug pellets and other garden chemicals.

- But there is hope. Some mammals, like otters and pine martens, have made a comeback in the UK now that we have started protecting them.

When it comes to hedgehogs, our towns and cities can provide just as safe a habitat as the countryside. Private gardens in the UK add up to a bigger area than all of its national nature reserves put together. As long as hedgehogs can access them, they can provide safe routes, or 'corridors', to travel along.

WHAT YOU'LL NEED

A TAPE MEASURE

A SPADE

A SAW AND A DRILL
(and an adult to help
you use them)

A PIECE OF PIPE
(optional)

STEP 1 – IDENTIFY YOUR SITE

- Look for an area of green space that is enclosed by walls or wooden fences that prevent hedgehogs from passing through to another area of green space. For example, this could be from your garden to a next-door-neighbour's garden, a local park or at your school.

IMPORTANT

Make sure you find out who owns the fence and get permission first (see page 191 in the 'Tips and Tricks' chapter for guidance).

TIP Hedgehogs hibernate from around October through to April so you will only see them in the summer months. Look at the Hedgehog Street Map online for signs of hedgehogs in your area.

- If there is already evidence of hedgehogs using the area, such as footprints, droppings or disturbed leaves and twigs on one side of the fence or wall, then you have found the perfect spot. You won't always know if hedgehogs are in the area; it might be that they are going undetected.

- If there are no physical signs or sightings recorded on the Hedgehog Street Map and there are also large numbers of badgers in the area, then you might have a problem as badgers can eat hedgehogs and compete with them for food. If this is the case you might want to explore another site.

STEP 2 – MAKE A PLAN

- Decide where you want to create a hedgehog hole in the fence or wall. It will need to be at ground level, around 13–15 cm high and wide enough to allow a hedgehog to pass through.

- What is your wall or fence made of? If it is a brick wall, you might need to remove some bricks. If it is a wooden fence, cut a hole. Or you can dig a small tunnel underneath either of these and use a piece of pipe to create a nice solid tunnel.

- Ask an adult, such as a parent or teacher, to help you choose the safest method.
- Make a list of all the tools you'll need and where you can get them from.

IMPORTANT

Ask an adult to help when using tools to cut or dig your hole.

STEP 3 – GATHER YOUR MATERIALS AND MAKE YOUR HEDGEHOG HOLE

- Measure your hole with a tape measure and draw the shape on to the wall or fence with a pencil. Or put a marker in the ground to mark where you want to dig under it.
- Cut or dig your hole and insert the pipe if you are using one.
- Put some soil or dry leaves around the base of your hole so that the hedgehogs will have an easy time travelling through.

TIP

Look at the Hedgehog Street website to see pictures of different hedgehog highways!

- To make sure people know why the hole is there, make a sign to hang above your hedgehog highway.

STEP 4 – ENCOURAGE HEDGEHOGS TO VISIT

- Create some nice hiding places with piles of dry leaves in a quiet corner near your hedgehog hole to make it an attractive spot for them to visit.

- You can even build a simple hedgehog home by creating a 13–15 cm hole in an upturned box and placing dry leaves inside.

- If there are signs of hedgehogs already, you can encourage them to use the hole by putting out some fresh water and dog or cat food (making sure it doesn't contain fish) or a chopped boiled egg for them to eat.

- Make sure that no slug pellets or other harmful pesticides are being used.

- If there is a pond nearby, make sure there is a way for them to climb out if they fall in.

- Keep an eye on the hole between April and October to see if it's being used!

- Extend your approach to improve other corridors in your area and create a wildlife network using Action 9 on page 51.

WHAT WILL IT ACHIEVE?

Imagine if all parks and gardens were linked and open to small mammals like hedgehogs so that they could move through them to find food and make homes – they would thrive!

ACTION 9   BUILD A NETWORK OF WILDLIFE CORRIDORS

CONNECT UP DIFFERENT WILDLIFE AREAS WITH SAFE
GREEN CORRIDORS TO MAKE IT EASIER FOR WILDLIFE
TO LIVE AMONG US

WHY?

- As wildlife areas become more and more divided up by new houses, roads and farmland they become broken up and fragmented, like islands in a sea.

- Wildlife will often struggle to travel between these islands to find food and homes and so these fragmented habitats can be as big a cause of wildlife declines as habitat loss.

You can connect up different wildlife areas with safe corridors so that species can move freely to find food and shelter, helping reverse nature's decline.

STEP 1 – MAPPING

- Decide on the size of your project area.

- Look at what existing wildlife areas there are where you live – these are the bigger parks, nature reserves and woodlands that are likely to provide a good habitat for different species.

- Use an online map to start to identify and record wildlife spaces in your area.

If you live in London, then luckily Kabir Kaul has already worked hard to create an incredible map of its wildlife spaces. Whether or not you live in London, use Kabir's map as an example and read his helpful blog, *Kaul of the Wild*, for an explanation of how he created his map and what the different types of nature site mean.

- Visit some of these places so that you understand them better and survey what wildlife already exists there (see Action 2 on page 8 for help).

- How do these bigger green spaces you've found join up? Are there corridors between them?

To find corridors, look for:
- rivers or streams
- hedgerows, rooftop gardens, road verges or lines of gardens
- railway lines with green banks
- field edges, ditches, avenues of trees, tunnels and underpasses
- abandoned building sites filled with weeds.

- Start to highlight these on your map like a network connecting the bigger wildlife areas.

- Once you have identified corridors on the map, go out and explore how your networks work in real life.

- Look for how an animal might pass through each corridor. Are there plenty of gaps in fences? Is the stream clean or full of litter? Is there good vegetation cover where animals can hide as they move along? Note down what you find.
- Now that you have done some research on the ground, colour code each corridor on your map:
  - Use green if it is a healthy corridor with good vegetation cover that is easy to move through.
  - Orange if it is good in some areas but difficult for some species to pass through in other places.
  - Red if the corridor is difficult to pass through and has poor-quality vegetation cover.

STEP 2 – PLANNING

- For each orange and red corridor, write down what you would need to do to turn it into a green corridor on your map. For example, do you need to create holes in fences (see Action 8 on page 46), do a litter pick, plant trees or generally rewild the corridor? Use other actions in this chapter to help you decide what needs to change and plan how to do it.
- Decide how much time improving each corridor will take and whether you can start right away or if you will need to wait until a specific time of year.
- Identify what materials you will need and where you can source them, and who owns the land, and build a team who can help you (use the 'Tips and Tricks' chapter on pages 188, 191 and 193).

STEP 3 – CONVINCING

- It is important to convince others, and particularly those who own the land, of the value of your actions.
- This might be simpler where there is one owner, and perhaps more complicated when you have multiple homeowners with individual gardens that need connecting up.

- Create a clear and compelling case for why you want more wildlife corridors. Explain why creating habitats that are connected is important for tackling wildlife declines.

- Share your research and copies of your maps. Outline why the land they own is so important for connecting bigger wildlife areas and what you'd like to do to improve the corridor for wildlife.

- If you get a positive response from a landowner, meet with them to make the case in person and agree a timeline for taking action (see page 192 in the 'Tips and Tricks' chapter).

- Be prepared to have discussions, be adaptable and change your plans.

- If you get a negative response, or no response at all, leave this corridor and focus on others.

STEP 4 – GET STARTED

- Finalize your plans.

- Draw up a schedule for getting the work done and begin improving your corridors with your team.

- Monitor your progress and adapt your plans where necessary.

- As always, remember to be kind to yourself. You are doing something ambitious and things won't always go the way you planned. Don't give up and, you never know, exciting, unexpected outcomes might happen too!

STEP 5 – NEXT STEPS

- Start a campaign to persuade reluctant landowners to give you permission to create corridors (look at page 152 for tips on setting up your campaign and deciding on aims and tactics).

- Share your approach to creating wildlife corridors or upload your map for others to use on the internet.

- Create some information boards to identify your corridors and inspire and educate others with vlogs, maps or even QR codes linked to a website about your corridors.

WHAT WILL IT ACHIEVE?

If everyone in the UK created a one-metre length of wildlife corridor, we would have enough to stretch around the Earth almost twice! Instead of being islands stuck in a sea of concrete, all our most important wildlife areas would become connected by a rich web of wildlife highways that allow animals to move freely.

CHAPTER 2   CLEAN AIR

ANDRE'S STORY

'If everyone is unique and brings their personality, we can solve the problem in different ways.'
ANDRE LUNT

PHOTO © NICOLE LUNT

Andre Lunt sat with his eyes fixed on the screen. The rest of his Year 8 Geography class seemed to fade away as he became more absorbed in the film. Until this point, he hadn't been aware of the scale of the climate crisis and what it meant for people around the world today. He hadn't realized that so many environmental problems are linked to social problems that have consequences for people. He felt inspired when activists talked about how they were facing up to these problems.

At the end of the lesson, the teacher announced that the school would be participating in a workshop programme on the environment. She explained that all the students involved would be supported in creating their own environmental projects. Andre liked the sound of this. Perhaps it could help him become an activist.

After joining the first workshop, Andre and his friends decided that they wanted to hold a walk-to-school day to raise awareness of air pollution and encourage sustainable forms of transport. Students who wanted to participate would be encouraged to donate to charity and allowed to wear their own clothes rather than their school uniform.

Their first step was to speak to the head teacher and get permission. He heard them out, but he said no. The uniform was non-negotiable. Time for a rethink. What if students who took part could wear trainers? That could be enough of an incentive. To give themselves the best chance of success they spoke to their Geography teacher and persuaded her to email the head teacher just before they asked again. Success. He said yes on the condition that it was just trainers.

The event would be called Happy Shoes Day. They put up posters all around school. When the day arrived, sixth formers helped supervise the different routes to school. Over a thousand young people walked and they raised £500 for charity. Happy Shoes Day was a success!

Next Andre's team thought about other ways to inspire students and educate them at the same time. They decided to create a poster competition on sustainable transport. The winner would receive a new bike as a prize. Andre found it tough convincing someone to give them a bike for free. He emailed lots of different businesses and charities. He persisted, ignoring all the organizations that said no, and eventually a local cycling group offered to donate a bike. The competition was a triumph and the winning poster is still on display in his school.

Andre's team were so successful that they were selected to attend an event with other schools participating in the environmental workshop programme across the city. They presented their project to a panel of judges and won second prize for their achievements. Andre's team continued to meet. Now their group has grown from four to 20. They discuss what community level action they can take to tackle climate breakdown. They plan to visit primary schools and talk about sustainable transport. They are even planning Happy Shoes Day Two!

The members of Andre's group inspire each other to do more, just like the activists in the film. Andre has volunteered at a local National Trust property, taking practical action for nature. He helped maintain and create wildlife habitats and look after young trees that had been planted there. Now 14, Andre wants to develop his confidence in public speaking and speak up in campaigns on climate justice for those in communities who are suffering the consequences of global heating.

ANDRE'S MESSAGE TO YOU

Whatever issue you are working hard to tackle, be yourself and bring your own interests into it. Don't get caught up in what the media or other people say, or how they say it. If everyone is saying the same thing it won't solve all aspects of the problem. If everyone is unique and brings their personality, we can solve the problem in different ways.

ACTION 10   PEDAL POWER

HOW TO START A SCHOOL CYCLING OR WALKING GROUP
AND AVOID CARS ALTOGETHER

WHY?

- Cars are a major cause of air pollution and greenhouse gas emissions.

The good news is that every time we walk or cycle instead of drive, we are reducing emissions, air pollution and traffic congestion. Here's how you can join Andre and help!

STEP 1 – GET A GROUP TOGETHER

- Speak to friends about the problem.
- Suggest a cycling or walking group and ensure you involve enough people so that there will always be more than one cyclist or walker (8–10 should be enough).
- Plan a route and meeting points and times.

STEP 2 – MAKE THE CASE

- Write a short paragraph proposal explaining what you want to do, who is involved, how you want to do it and why it is important.
- Discuss the idea with your head teacher and ask them to write a letter of support to each of your parents or guardians.
- Ask permission from your parent or guardian to cycle or walk.

STEP 3 – GET THE GEAR AND STAY SAFE

- If you are cycling, make sure every member of the group has the right equipment and is aware of road safety.

HERE'S WHAT YOU'LL NEED TO CYCLE:

- A bike that has been serviced
- A helmet
- Bike lights
- A reflective vest
- A bike lock
- Waterproof clothing.

- You might be able to find organizations you can approach which will service your bike for free or give advice – take a look online.
- If anyone in your group needs to buy a second-hand bike you can raise money for the project (see page 198 in the 'Tips and Tricks' chapter).

STEP 4 – GET ORGANIZED

- Set up a WhatsApp or email group and use it to organize and plan your trips.
- You can also create a notice board at school to let other members of the group know when you plan to cycle or walk. This will also help advertise your campaign to other students.
- Practise your route and check the meeting times – does it work or do you need to change the time or route to avoid busy roads or traffic?

TIP Sometimes it's better to take a slightly longer route if it is less busy.

STEP 5 – NEXT STEPS

- Calculate the number of miles cycled or walked and the carbon emissions saved in your first month and share it with your school so that other students and parents can hear about what you are doing.

Greenhouse gas emissions are expressed as grams of CO_2 equivalent (CO_2e). One mile on a bike saves around 620 g of CO_2e, compared to the same distance in a car.

- Speak at a school assembly about your success and create a leaflet or downloadable map of the safest routes to engage other students and recruit more cycling or walking groups.
- Take your campaign to the next level by working to reduce car use in your local area and promote walking, cycling and public transport using Action 28 on page 165.

WHAT WILL IT ACHIEVE?

Just think, if ten of you cycled one mile, three times a week for a year instead of driving, you could save the equivalent CO_2e of a return flight from London to New York. You would be fitter and healthier too. The more you cycle, the bigger your positive impact!

ACTION 11 — CAR STAR

SET UP A LIFT-SHARE SCHEME WITH OTHER STUDENTS TO REDUCE THE NUMBER OF CAR JOURNEYS TO SCHOOL

WHY?

- Globally, around a quarter of our CO_2 emissions come from transport.
- In the UK, transport is now the biggest source of CO_2 emissions.
- Cars are a major cause of air pollution, and dirty air causes seven million early deaths a year.

Every time we share trips in a car, we reduce our carbon footprint and help to tackle this global problem.

STEP 1 – GET A GROUP

- Identify a group of friends at school who all live near you.
- Suggest creating a lift-share scheme and involve enough people to fill a car.

STEP 2 – MAKE THE CASE

- Get your friends to discuss the idea with the people who drive them to school. If they agree to become involved, find out which days they would prefer to drive everyone.
- Work out a rota for which adults are driving and when and where the pick-up points will be.

TIP

One parent or guardian is most likely going to have to drive twice in one week, as the average car only carries four passengers but there are five days in the week. You can change this weekly so that this responsibility is shared and you will need to be flexible to take account of after-school clubs.

STEP 3 – GET ORGANIZED

- Draw up a timetable for the next month showing who is driving when and then share this with your drivers to confirm they are happy with the arrangement.

- Make sure to include details on times and pick-up locations on the timetable. You could also include a series of tips for low emissions driving.

TIPS FOR LOW EMISSIONS DRIVING TO SHARE WITH ADULTS:

- Drive a smaller more efficient car – up to 50% saving.
- Keep the car well serviced and tyres at the right pressure. This will also be safer. Around 30% saving.
- Try to avoid braking heavily in urban areas by accelerating and decelerating gently – up to 20% saving.

- Set up a WhatsApp or email group and make sure everyone has access so that you can notify everyone if arrangements need to change.

- Practise your route and the meeting times – does it work or do you need to change the time or route to arrive on time?

STEP 4 – RECORD YOUR IMPACT

- Start monitoring how many journeys you have saved; in the first week this could be as many as 30 journeys to or from school!

- Record this on a spreadsheet and start calculating the carbon emissions you have avoided and how much money hasn't been spent on fuel – you can find online calculators to help you work out how much money you have saved. Let your drivers know the results and thank them for their help too.

HOW TO CALCULATE YOUR CARBON SAVINGS BY LIFT SHARING

An average car uses 710 g CO_2e to travel a mile. If your school is five miles away then by going in one car rather than four separate cars, you would save 106.5 kg CO_2e in a week of return journeys. This is almost as much as a return train journey from London to Glasgow. After four weeks, travelling to and from school, you would save 426 kg of CO_2e, almost as much as a return flight from London to Glasgow!

STEP 5 – NEXT STEPS

- Write a letter to your head teacher about your lift-share scheme and how much you have saved in carbon emissions and the benefits for air quality.

- Write an article about your scheme in the school newsletter so that other students and parents hear about what you are doing. You can also create a notice board at school about it.

- Now that you have got the attention of students at your school, take this to the next level and help other groups set up a similar scheme or launch a campaign to reduce car use in your local area (find out how to set up your campaign on page 152 and use Action 28 on page 165 for detailed campaign tips).

WHAT WILL IT ACHIEVE?

If you were to run your lift-share scheme for a whole school year, an average of 190 school days, assuming a travel distance per day of five miles each way, then you would save 4.047 tonnes of CO_2e, which is the equivalent of a return flight from London to Hong Kong. You will also be helping reduce air pollution in your local area, benefitting people's health too!

CHAPTER 3   FOOD

ACTION 12   EAT GREEN

HELP THE PLANET BY REDUCING THE AMOUNT OF MEAT,
FISH, EGGS AND DAIRY YOU EAT OR BY GOING VEGETARIAN
OR VEGAN WITH YOUR FAMILY

WHY?

- Rearing animals for food is one of the leading causes of habitat loss. It uses huge amounts of water and it is a big source of pollution and greenhouse gas emissions.

- Almost 80% of all farmland in the world is used for rearing animals for meat or growing crops to feed them.

- With overfishing, wild fish populations could collapse by 2050, leaving millions of people without their main source of protein and causing a catastrophic extinction crisis in our oceans.

Eating less meat, fish, eggs and dairy in favour of sustainable alternatives is one of the quickest and biggest changes we can make to our environmental impact as individuals.

STEP 1 – RESEARCH

- First you need to find out why reducing meat, fish, eggs and dairy is good for the environment and for our health – research it online and come up with a list of 8–10 reasons, starting with some of the facts above.

Certain kinds of meat production might be less harmful than others. For instance, chicken production typically has a lower environmental impact than beef production, but locally grown grass-fed organic beef could have less of an impact than beef flown from another country with high deforestation rates and better welfare standards than battery chicken farms. Some meat- and dairy-free alternatives can have high environmental impacts too, depending on where and how the ingredients are grown. The choice is rarely simple, so make sure you do your research!

- Think about who your family members respect, like friends or celebrities, and find out which ones are vegetarian or vegan. These examples will be helpful when convincing your family to trial a meat-free diet.

STEP 2 – MEAL PLAN

- Start by recording what you eat over a whole week, draw a lamb chop, fish, egg or a milk carton symbol next to meals where you have had meat, fish, eggs or dairy.

- Take your weekly meal plan and create a new version where you start substituting meat and fish (if you want to try a vegetarian diet) and eggs and dairy (if you want to move towards a vegan diet) for other ingredients or changing whole meals to something different.

- Explore different recipes. Look online and in cookbooks. Pick things that sound exciting and that you would like to eat.

- Try to avoid overly elaborate meals with expensive or hard-to-find ingredients.

There are lots of meat and dairy alternatives available, but be aware that some are heavily processed and can be bad for the environment too. Keep it as local and fresh as you can. You can look online for information on achieving a balanced diet and meeting your nutritional needs while avoiding or reducing the use of animal products. For example, the World Wide Fund for Nature's (WWF) Livewell report looks at the diet we need to follow to keep global heating in check.

WEEKLY FOOD PLAN

FIRST WEEK				
MONDAY				
TUESDAY				
WEDNESDAY				
THURSDAY				
FRIDAY				
SATURDAY				
SUNDAY				

NEW MEAL PLAN WITH SUBSTITUTIONS

STEP 3 – COMPARE PRICES

- Next to each meal in both meal plans write down all the ingredients and rough amounts needed (as if you were creating an ingredients list for a recipe).

- Take your two meal plans and look online or in person in the shop where you buy most of your food and calculate the cost of all the ingredients. Don't forget to use Action 14 on page 83 to look for more sustainable options for your new meal plan too.

- What does it add up to? Sometimes more sustainable options can have a higher price tag, but meat, fish, eggs and dairy can be expensive too, so you might find that, even with more sustainable options in your new meal plan, it is cheaper or similar to your original shop.

STEP 4 – MAKE THE CASE AND GIVE IT A GO

- Present your research and cost comparisons to your family. Explain that you would like to trial your new meal plan for a week.

- If you are having trouble persuading your family, then offer to help with the cooking for the week or to do all the washing up (maybe save that one until last!).

- Once they have agreed, help do the shopping to buy the food, prepare your recipes and get cooking.

- After each meal, ask everyone what they thought and write this down.

- At the end of the trial week, present your family with their feedback, and ask whether they would consider extending the trial, reducing the amount of meat, fish, eggs and dairy or cutting them out altogether.

STEP 5 – NEXT STEPS

- After a month follow the first bullet point in Step 2 again to track what your family is eating over a week. How does this compare to your diet before you took this action? How does it compare to the meal plan you trialled in the first week? Could improvements be made? Is it time to push your family to go further? Do the same after six months and then a year.

- Look at Action 14 on page 83 and continue to evaluate the food you or your family are buying and eating and make sure it is sustainable.

WHAT WILL IT ACHIEVE?

By eating a vegetarian diet for a year, a family of four would reduce their carbon emissions by as much as if they were to stop driving a car for almost a year. This diet would also use much less water and need less land to produce the food that was eaten, reducing pressure on wildlife around the globe.

LOUISE'S STORY

'Together we can change the world.'
LOUISE CHAUVET

Six-year-old Louise Chauvet picked up a plastic bottle. The label had long been washed away by the ocean. The plastic had turned a milky colour, like the foam-topped waves that had carried it to the beach. Wide-eyed, she looked around at the amount of litter her community had collected along the beach in just one afternoon. Living on the Isle of Mull, an island off the west coast of Scotland, she had thought that she was far away from this kind of problem.

When she got a little older, Louise started to visit the island's aquarium. The aquarium is special. It is the first catch and release aquarium in Europe, where all the marine animals in the tanks are returned to the ocean after no more than four weeks. She learnt all about life in the sea. She was fascinated by the starfish in particular. She started to explore the coastline, where she found a sea cave full of starfish. Louise couldn't let plastic destroy the sea and these special creatures. It was time to organize some more regular beach cleans with her friends and family. Together they would spread the word on social media and by making posters.

After completing an environmental award scheme, called the John Muir Award, with her brother, James, Louise was inspired to explore ways of educating other young people.

With her mum and her brother, she has helped over 180 children complete the award, teaching them how to protect nature in the process. Drawn by her love of the ocean, Louise attended a workshop run by the Hebridean Whale and Dolphin Trust. She learnt all about their Whale Track app (which you can use to record sightings of whales and dolphins) and they invited her and her brother back to run a workshop with other children. She even created a game to teach other children how to identify these beautiful creatures.

At the age of 12, Louise started to become more aware of climate breakdown and began to explore ways that she could reduce her carbon footprint. The most obvious place to start was with the food that she and her family ate. Because Mull is an island, most of the food for sale in the shops has to be transported from the mainland by ferry. To preserve it, much of the food is wrapped in plastic. This didn't seem right, Louise thought; perhaps she could grow some of her own food.

Louise joined a local project called Grow, Grow, Grow. They look for empty spaces behind churches and community halls and use them to grow fruit and vegetables that are then sold at local markets. Over the next 18 months Louise became more and more involved in helping grow the produce. With the experience she gained, she started her own vegetable garden with her family. She created vegetable beds, and designated a space for wild flowers to help pollinating insects. Now 13, Louise plans to feed her family with the food she grows.

LOUISE'S MESSAGE TO YOU

Change starts with you. Small steps lead to big steps. Talk to everyone about what you do and why it is important. It will give you confidence. Together we can change the world.

ACTION 13 · GROW YOUR OWN FOOD

START GROWING YOUR OWN VEGETABLES LIKE LOUISE!

WHY?

- 40–50% of the food we eat in the UK comes from abroad and food that travels further before it reaches our plate can have a bigger carbon footprint.

- By growing some of your own food, you not only reduce greenhouse gas emissions, but you can avoid using harmful pesticides and fertilizers that damage wildlife and are unhealthy for you.

- You will be creating a cheap source of good food for you, your friends and family and space for wildlife to thrive at the same time.

You can grow food wherever you live. For inspiration, just google Ron Finley's TED talk to see how one person has become a 'Gangsta Gardener' and made a difference through urban gardening.

WHAT YOU'LL NEED

PEAT-FREE COMPOST

ORGANIC FERTILIZER

GARDEN TOOLS

SEEDS

OLD TOILET ROLL
TUBES OR EGG BOXES

MATERIALS, SUCH AS WOOD
(optional)

STEP 1 – FIND A PLACE TO GROW

- Look for a place to grow. It doesn't have to be big; in fact it is better to start small. You could start with some recycled plastic bottle planters on a windowsill or balcony (see Action 5 on page 27 for inspiration), use space in your garden or a friend's or look for a space at school.

- Think about practicalities, like how you will get access to water for watering your plants and where you will store tools at night.

- Once you've made a list of potential sites, take your top pick and get permission to grow there (see page 191 in the 'Tips and Tricks' chapter for advice on how to get permission). If you can't grow there, go to the next site on your list until you've found one that's possible.

STEP 2 – PLAN YOUR PLANTING

- Decide which crops you want to plant.

- Could you put together a team to help? (See page 193 in the 'Tips and Tricks' chapter for a guide.) If you are in the UK, you could even set up or link in with 'Incredible Edible' groups in your area. Their website has lots of helpful resources too.

- If you are involving others, the whole team can ask around and find out what kind of vegetables are preferred by family members and friends. You could start with these.

- Try to pick a range of crops that you can sow (plant seeds) and harvest (pick) at different times of year, so that you always have something growing. Incredible Edible has a helpful crop planner and other guides, which is a great place to start.

- Decide on a shortlist of 8–10 crops and research growing each of them on the internet. Some crops might do less well in the space you plan to plant them in, so be prepared to exchange a few of your choices for others.

- You could create one-page growing guides for different crops, explaining what the crop is, how you plant it, how you care for it and when and how you pick it. If you have a team, each person can do one or two crops each.

- Decide how you are going to plant – is it straight into the ground or in pots?

- Plan how you will water your crops. Most will need regular watering, so make sure you have time for this or create a rota if you are gardening in a team.

- Your plants will come under attack from a range of hungry animals like slugs, snails, rabbits and caterpillars. The crops you have chosen might be a favourite food for particular species. Spend time researching environmentally friendly alternatives to chemical pesticides online – there are lots of options. Practise acceptance; you will lose some crops – think of it as nature's share.

STEP 3 – SOURCE YOUR SEEDS AND MATERIALS

- See page 188 in the 'Tips and Tricks' chapter for guidance on sourcing materials, seeds and tools.

- Ask for advice on crop varieties and types of compost at your local garden centre. Remember to ensure your compost is peat-free, though.

- There is a lot of information online on creating seed trays using old toilet roll tubes, egg boxes and even newspaper.

 You don't have to grow crops from seed; it can be easier to get seedlings (baby plants) to start with.

STEP 4 – GET GROWING

- Start by growing your seeds in seed trays, following the instructions on the packet or using your growing guides and any information you have found online.

- In the meantime, prepare your growing space ready for planting outdoors. Dig the soil and add the peat-free compost and organic fertilizer according to the instructions.

- Once the seeds grow into seedlings, plant them in your prepared soil and place a marker with the name of what you planted next to them so you know what is where.

- Implement your natural pest control strategies that you researched in Step 2 and use Action 5 on page 27 to plant some pollinator-friendly flowers at your site too.

- Water and care for your plants as they grow.

- When your crops are ready, harvest and eat them! It is hard to put into words how much of an achievement this is or to overestimate the sense of success you will feel.

- Don't forget to look online at how to collect seed from your plants so that you will have free seeds forever!

STEP 5 – NEXT STEPS

- Celebrate the harvesting of your crops by holding a communal meal or a party – harvest festivals have been around for thousands of years. Reinvent it and make it relevant to you and your community.

- If you manage to grow more food than you can eat yourselves, you could start donating produce or even selling some of it to your local community and use the money to help fund your garden.

- Expand your operations and grow your group. Are there other people you could involve? Is there space to expand at your current site or could you start a second site or move location?

WHAT WILL IT ACHIEVE?

Your garden will be a source of fresh, organic, local food. That alone will have a big impact on the environment. But watch how the action of growing food will inspire others too. By growing crops you will plant seeds of change in the people around you.

ACTION 14 | FOOD FOR THOUGHT

DESIGN A GUIDE TO SUSTAINABLE FOOD CHOICES

- -

WHY?

- The way we produce food has a big impact on nature. Agriculture uses 34% of our land and 69% of our water and has caused 75% of deforestation and 70% of biodiversity loss globally.

- We throw away around a third of all food we produce, yet across the world one in nine people are hungry.

- As our global population grows from 7.7 to 9.7 billion people in the next 30 years, we simply cannot afford to go on producing food in the way we do. We need to create a more sustainable food system.

As individuals we may not feel that we can change things, but when it comes to our food, we are an integral part of the system – every single person has to eat. Help other people drive change through more sustainable food choices.

STEP 1 – CREATE A STRUCTURE

- Develop a structure for your guide.

- Make it easy for people to use. You could have sections on different food types, like meat, fish and vegetables.

WHAT IS CERTIFICATION?

- Schemes like the Soil Association's Organic Certification, the Marine Stewardship Council (MSC) and Fairtrade show us that companies and products meet certain environmental or sustainability standards and that farmers receive a fair wage. Look out for their logos on products.

- While none of these schemes is perfect and there are always improvements to be made, it is definitely a start.

- There are other important considerations like buying local and seasonal produce and avoiding food that has a large amount of packaging.

- You might find you want sections on the importance of reducing meat, dairy, egg and fish consumption, certification, or how sustainable it is to grow your own fruit and vegetables.

- The cost of food is another thing to think about, including how and where to find organic products cheaply, how to keep costs down when buying ethically or which restaurants to eat at.

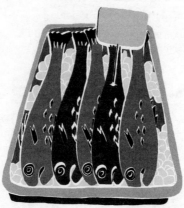

EXAMPLE SUSTAINABLE FOOD GUIDE STRUCTURE

Don't feel you have to stick to this example structure. Design something that will work for you and, more importantly, something that will work for the people you want to use it!

- Introduction – why sourcing sustainably is important for the environment, including a note on food costs and how to keep costs down
- Section 1: Sourcing local, seasonal produce
- Section 2: Buying organic food
- Section 3: How you know products are sustainable; certification and key food groups
- Section 4: The importance of diet and dietary changes
- Section 5: Minimizing packaging and food waste
- Section 6: Where to shop and eat out
- Conclusion – motivational last words encouraging people to join you in spreading the word, sharing the guide and making more sustainable food choices.

STEP 2 – DO YOUR RESEARCH

- It is easiest to break your research down into manageable chunks, by looking at one section at a time.

TIP Food sustainability is a huge topic. No one person has all the knowledge or all the answers, so don't expect to get everything right.

- Pick information that is most relevant to you and your community. Perhaps there are particular foods your family or friends like to eat, for instance, or maybe food waste is a particular issue at your school.

- A great place to start is with resources listed on the Sustain website. Sustain is a group of around a hundred organizations working to make food and farming more sustainable. Ethical Consumer produces guides to particular brands and ranks their sustainability.

- There are also apps and guides for specific food types. For example, the Marine Conservation Society's *Good Fish Guide* is a great place to explore the sustainability of fish and seafood.

STEP 3 – PUT IT TOGETHER

- Write the text for each section. Use bullet points and keep text short and simple.

- Focus on how the reader will use the information and tailor it to them. In every section, make sure you give practical steps that your readers can take.

- Write the introduction and conclusion last, so that you have a good overview of everything in the guide first.

- When you have finished writing, design the guide.

- Create an eye-catching front page and a mixture of text and images throughout to get people's attention. Make sure you use your own photos or look online for copyright-free images that you can use without payment.

- Test your first draft out on friends or family members and ask for their feedback.

- Create a final draft and check it over one last time for mistakes.

- Will you keep your guide digital or are you going to print hard copies? How many copies will you need? (See page 190 in the 'Tips and Tricks' chapter about printing and paper.)

STEP 4 – SHARE AND EMPOWER

- You want people to act on the advice you give in your guide, so make sure you present your message in a way that doesn't make them feel guilty.

- Talk to people about what's in the guide. Encourage them to start with one section and see how it goes.

- Review your guide in the light of any feedback you get, or new information you find out. It may become clear that there are improvements you could make.

STEP 5 – NEXT STEPS

- Use all the knowledge you have gained and the information you have collected to start a food-related campaign using Action 33 on page 180 or Action 34 on page 182.

WHAT WILL IT ACHIEVE?

Driving change in our food system is critical if we are to avoid catastrophic impacts on our environment. If your guide can persuade just a handful of people to change to more sustainable eating habits, think about what a positive impact this will have over the course of their lifetime as they buy, grow and eat food.

CHAPTER 4 THROW-AWAY CULTURE

LILY'S STORY

'Put yourself out there, read as much as you can and ask lots of questions, but above all, take action.'

LILY MACFARLANE

PHOTO © CALEB MARCHENT

Lily Macfarlane looked out as the shadows of the clouds danced across the surface of the sea far down below. A bird rose on the wind and then dropped under the edge of the cliff. It was beautiful. She had just arrived in Wales on a trip to learn about the environment with a group of other young people and she didn't know what to expect. But in that moment, she felt a sense of wonder, hope and urgency like never before.

Back home in Cambridge, Lily looked at her city with new eyes. She began to work on tackling the issue that felt closest to her everyday life first – the problem of plastic. She could see in the news how important this problem was to her generation. The sea, which she had been sitting and watching from high up on the cliff top, could contain a greater weight of plastic than fish by the year 2050. She couldn't let this happen.

Lily wanted to communicate her concerns to other young people. Her love of art inspired her to create a short video of herself drawing a plastic bottle with the earth inside it. She wrote a script to read out as she drew and the picture revealed itself. Her short film was released on Twitter and it went viral overnight! Teachers got in touch to say they were using it in their lessons, environmental charities asked if they could share it with their supporters. Young people she knew started to take notice of the problem. Lily felt motivated to take further action for wildlife and the environment.

Lily travelled to Southampton to volunteer for a day helping monitor vital populations of native oysters and attended her first protest march, the Walk for Wildlife. Back home she started volunteering at a community garden in a local park, planting wild flower beds and growing fruit and vegetables. She even helped build a pond and homes for insects. Amazed by all these beautiful and weird creatures she had never noticed before, Lily wanted to tell their story.

She decided to open her pencil case again, this time to tell the world about the tansy beetle. The very existence of this iridescent, blue-green marvel is under threat in the UK. In this video, Lily decided to start with the completed drawing of a colourful tansy beetle. As she talked about catastrophic declines in wildlife, the film ran backwards and her drawing process was reversed so that the picture of the beetle disappeared. Just as the last pencil lines were fading, she began to explain what we can do for nature to reverse these losses. The film ran forward again, showing her creating the drawing, and the tansy beetle sprung back to life. Her film captured people's hearts. Young people and school teachers across the UK, and even as far away as North America and Pakistan, got in touch with Lily to ask if they could share it. The charity Greenpeace included a link to her film in their newsletter.

Now Lily has turned her attention to fast fashion. She was shocked to find out how regularly cheap clothes are bought and discarded and the impact that our clothes addiction has on the planet: plastic microfibre pollution; vast amounts of water used to grow cotton; toxic chemical dyes that pollute the environment; child labour; and poor welfare for workers. All these big global problems, just so we can keep up with the latest fashion trends. From then on she decided to buy only second-hand clothes and she launched a pop-up swap shop for used clothes at her school for a week. Now she wants to open up her pencil case for a third time and create a film on fast fashion. Watch out, fashion industry, you are about to get stitched up.

LILY'S MESSAGE TO YOU

We are at a key moment in history, a window of opportunity to act. We have to drive change on three levels. There are the personal changes, like diet or avoiding plastic, the changes in organizations and institutions like schools and there is political change. Put yourself out there, read as much as you can and ask lots of questions, but above all, take action. Together we can bring about change at all three levels.

ORGANIZE A CLOTHING SWAP SHOP LIKE LILY!

- -

WHY?

- Around the world, the equivalent of a rubbish truck full of clothes is burnt or sent to landfill every second.

- It takes 2,700 litres of water to make just one cotton shirt, usually in countries that suffer from drought – this is the same amount as 2.5 years' worth of drinking water for one person.

- Polyester clothes are a major cause of microplastic pollution, with one wash releasing up to 700,000 microfibres into the environment. They are the leading cause of plastic in the air we all breathe.

By extending the life of our clothes through recycling, repurposing or buying second-hand, we can significantly reduce one of the biggest impacts we have on the planet.

WHAT YOU'LL NEED

A PLACE TO SET UP YOUR SHOP

A TABLE OR HANGING RAILS

DONATED CLOTHES

AN EXERCISE BOOK FOR KEEPING STOCK RECORDS

PAPER AND PRINTING FACILITIES

STEP 1 – BUILD A TEAM, FIND A SPOT
AND MAKE A PLAN

- Put together a team (see page 193 in the 'Tips and Tricks' chapter).

- Find space for your swap shop. It could be at home, school or even at the community centre. Just make sure to get permission before you do anything.

 See page 191 in the 'Tips and Tricks' chapter for help with getting permission.

- Pick a spot that is busy and that people can easily see and visit.

- Before you can officially open your shop and start swapping, you'll need to collect a stock of second-hand clothes. Think about what kind of clothes you want to trade (is there a particular style or theme?) and then advertise a period of time and a place for people to donate their unwanted clothes.

- You'll need to make sure the clothes are washed and find somewhere to display them, like a table or hanging rail, and store them when the shop is closed.

- Work out the opening hours for your shop. Then set up a shift rota for your team and anyone else who would like to volunteer – you can tempt volunteers by giving them first pick of items or an extra item when they make a swap.

STEP 2 – SPREAD THE WORD

- If your swap shop is at school, organize assemblies to explain your project. Give examples of celebrities who wear second-hand clothing, simple facts about the impact of clothing and fast fashion and explain your solution – a swap shop!

- Give your shop a catchy name – create a brand.

- Advertise with posters in school or do a fashion show or photoshoot to promote the shop.
- Ask your Geography or Science teachers to focus on the clothing industry as a case study over the next term.

STEP 3 – OPEN FOR BUSINESS

- Create a fun opening ceremony and cut the ceremonial second-hand ribbon.
- Think about some other stunts you can use to draw attention to your swap shop on launch day or in the first few weeks. A fashion show? A giveaway day?
- Create a clothes donation box.
- Get started swapping clothes. Keep a log of which clothes you have in stock and how many you have traded.
- Remember, the more stock you have and the better quality your stock is, the more popular your shop will be.

STEP 4 – NEXT STEPS

- Once your shop starts to create a name for itself, you can go bigger by adding other things that can be reused as well as clothes.
- If your shop really takes off, why not take it online and set up a website or a newsletter? (See Action 24 on page 135 for writing tips.)

WHAT WILL IT ACHIEVE?

If there are 1,000 students in your school and they all visited your swap shop once and bought just one less cotton T-shirt as a result, you would save 2.7 million litres of water. That represents a year's drinking water for 2,500 people in a country experiencing water scarcity!

ACTION 16 THROW-AWAY THREADS

DESIGN AND MAKE CLOTHING AND OTHER ITEMS FROM
RECYCLED PRODUCTS

WHY?

- Every year scientists calculate the date in the year when
  we have used a year's worth of resources; they call it 'Earth
  Overshoot Day'. In 2020, that day was 22 August. In eight
  months, we used twelve months' worth of resources.

We can't go on extracting, making, buying, using and
throwing away. There is another way, a circular economy where
we take what is old and make it new again – 'upcycling'. Let's
join the circle and bin throw-away culture for good.

>
> **TIP**
> You don't even need a sewing machine or special tools
> to start making new from old. Let your imagination run
> riot with scissors, needle and thread, and glue. You'll be
> surprised by what you can do.

WHAT YOU'LL NEED

OLD ITEMS OF
CLOTHING OR FABRIC

OTHER DISUSED HOUSEHOLD
ITEMS OR DISCARDED OR
BROKEN FURNITURE

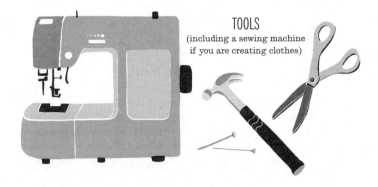

TOOLS
(including a sewing machine
if you are creating clothes)

STEP 1 – SCAVENGE MATERIALS

BEFORE YOU GET STARTED

There are two ways of looking at upcycling. The first is
that you scavenge for materials and then decide what to
make out of them. The second is to start with Step 2 of
this action and design what you want to make and then
look for materials to make it.

- Collect old or unwanted clothes or other materials and
  items around your house and local area.
- Store your finds and start thinking about what you
  might make.

STEP 2 – DECIDE ON DESIGNS

- Assess what you have collected and draw up some ideas.
  Try to be realistic.
- Look online to get inspired. Search 'upcycling ideas'.
- Try to find something you like, which will make good use of
  the things you have scavenged.

STEP 3 – PLAN IT OUT

- Identify any materials you are currently missing and think about where you might get hold of them (see page 188 in the 'Tips and Tricks' chapter for ideas on how to source materials).

- Assemble any tools you will need and decide if you are going to need help from someone with particular expertise, such as sewing or woodwork.

- Create a rough plan for your design and think about how long it will take to make.

STEP 4 – UPCYCLE

- It's time for your big creative experiment!

- Take your time to work things out as you go, but don't be too worried about changing the design if you encounter any difficulties.

IMPORTANT

Make sure you get an adult to help with any tools you use and that you are in a well-ventilated place if you are using paint or glue.

- Keep a note of things you would do differently next time around.

STEP 5 – NEXT STEPS

- Start selling upcycled items and make money for a charity or to fund other environmental projects (see page 198 in the 'Tips and Tricks' chapter for advice on fundraising).

- Start trading upcycled products through a swap shop using Action 15 on page 93.

- Expand your operations by setting up an upcycling group at school (see page 193 in the 'Tips and Tricks' chapter). Ask at school or a local community centre if they have a space for you to meet, work and store your materials as a group.

WHAT WILL IT ACHIEVE?

Every time you take something old and turn it into something new, you are avoiding sending it to landfill and helping to prevent pollution, resource extraction and carbon emissions caused by making a brand-new product!

ACTION 17 PLASTIC FREE

HOW TO ELIMINATE SINGLE-USE PLASTICS AT HOME

- -

WHY?

- Globally, we produce 300 million tonnes of plastic waste a year and eight million tonnes of this end up in our oceans. We have recycled just 9% of all the plastic that has ever been produced.

- Half of all plastic produced is designed to be used just once. For example, more than a million plastic bags are used every minute.

- Over 99% of plastics are made of chemicals that come from oil, natural gas or coal, and if trends continue, by 2050 plastic could account for 20% of the world's oil use.

IMPORTANT

Plastic does have some crucial uses, but most single-use plastics make no sense at all. They are damaging the planet.

You can help make single-use plastics a thing of the past.

STEP 1 – PLASTIC AUDIT

- Start by making an assessment of what single-use plastic you have at home.

- Note down what single-use plastic is used for and how frequently. Common uses are water bottles, food packaging, plastic bags, takeaway boxes and plastic straws.

STEP 2 – FIND ALTERNATIVES

- With each single-use plastic you have identified, research a few possible alternatives.

- For example, you could replace a plastic bottle with a reusable bottle or a plastic straw with a metal or bamboo straw, or no straw at all.

- Look for the cheapest source for all your new reusable items.

- When it comes to food with less packaging, look at where your family shops and investigate what plastic-free options there are, or look for other retailers who sell loose fruit and vegetables.

- You can also look at refillable options.

STEP 3 – MAKE THE CASE AT HOME

- Bring together all your research, your list of alternatives and the costs, together with some of the facts above.

- Present everything to your family. Explain that you would like to explore replacing single-use plastic at home. See how everyone responds.

- If you are having trouble persuading them, then offer to help with some chores in return for everyone trying it out!

- Once they have agreed, help with the shopping or online ordering and get everyone using the replacements.

- After a week, evaluate how it is going and discuss what improvements or changes you might all want to make.

- You are now ready to take the plastic challenge to a bigger stage – your school.

WHAT WILL IT ACHIEVE?

Eliminating or reducing single-use plastics at home is a huge, huge achievement for people and wildlife. The plastic crisis can feel overwhelming because of its scale, but by setting an example where you are, and by convincing others to change their behaviour, you are playing your part in driving a shift in mindset and in culture.

'Refuse what you can't reuse'.

ADITYA MUKARJI

PHOTO © ANUPAMA MUKARJI AND DEEPAK MUKARJI

The sea turtle moved its head from side to side and hissed as the biologist used pliers to pull at something poking out of its nose. Bit by bit a yellowy brown stick emerged. The turtle closed its eyes in distress. Finally, with one last tug it came out. A plastic straw. Fourteen-year-old Aditya Mukarji was sitting at a computer in his home, just outside Delhi, India, over a thousand kilometres from the sea, watching the story unfold. He couldn't believe it. How could it be that one small plastic straw, carelessly cast aside after it had been used just once, could do this much damage? One turtle, one straw. We throw away millions without thinking twice, he thought.

Aditya wanted to do something about this problem. He decided to focus on the hospitality sector – businesses like restaurants and hotels. He researched the problem and found out that as much as 50% of the plastic used in these businesses is single-use. He approached a hotel to discuss the problem with them. The hotel manager asked him an important question. What are the alternatives to these plastic products and where can I find them? Aditya did some research and found an Indian producer of paper, metal, bamboo and cornstarch straws. When he passed this on to the hotel manager, it wasn't long before he had convinced his first hotel to go single-use plastic straw free.

Over time more and more companies in India started to make plastic-free alternatives and Aditya started to make a list and use it to convince other businesses to go single-use plastic free. Aditya met with the President of the Market Association for a big market in central Delhi and secured the association's support for his campaign. He was then able to approach stalls and restaurants in the market and convince them to go single-use plastic free. After a year of persistence, he had converted 35 restaurants.

However, there were just a few big cafe chains that were resisting and making excuses. Aditya was determined. He continued to work hard. His mantra, 'refuse if you can't reuse', was spreading. He managed to convince a cinema chain, with 1,500 screens across India, to eliminate single-use plastic and turn any plastic waste they couldn't recycle into uniforms for their staff. He persuaded a hotel chain operating across India and internationally to get rid of single-use plastic straws. As of April 2019, he had eliminated 26 million plastic straws and convinced over 170 establishments to give up single-use plastics.

His campaign attracted attention from the media and international organizations. At 15, he was offered an internship at the UN Development Programme in India, making him the youngest intern in its 55-year history. The UN sponsored him to join the very first UN Youth Climate Summit in New York in September 2019. At the event, he was inspired by all the other young activists and it gave him an idea. The UN could appoint youth leaders in each country to engage young people at the grassroots level and drive positive change for the environment. Aditya hopes he can make it a reality.

ADITYA'S MESSAGE TO YOU

Refuse what you can't reuse, try to leave every place a little better than you found it and remember, no action is too big or too small. It all goes towards the greater good of the planet.

ACTION 18 DON'T BOTTLE IT

JOIN ADITYA AND GET ALL STUDENTS AT YOUR SCHOOL TO USE REUSABLE WATER BOTTLES

WHY?

- One million plastic bottles are bought per minute globally, and the average plastic bottle takes 450 years to biodegrade. Some bottles could take 1,000 years.

- As plastics break down into smaller and smaller pieces, or microplastics, they make their way into everything. Microplastic is found in the majority of tap water across the world and is consumed by animals we then eat.

- Plastic waste kills up to a million seabirds each year and, by weight, there could be more plastic than fish in the ocean by 2050 unless we do something about this problem.

The good news is that every time you drink from a reusable water bottle you avoid adding one more plastic bottle to the world.

STEP 1 – GATHER EVIDENCE

- Do a series of litter picks on your school grounds over a period of a week and count how many single-use plastic bottles and cups you collect.

HOW MANY BOTTLES DID YOU COLLECT?

- Speak to your school catering department and ask if they know how many water bottles are ordered and sold on a weekly/monthly/yearly basis.
- Calculate how much CO_2e was emitted when making this many bottles by multiplying the number of bottles by the average production cost for one 500 ml bottle, 160 g CO_2e.

WRITE DOWN THE CO_2e FOR THE NUMBER OF BOTTLES SOLD IN THE CANTEEN ON A WEEKLY/MONTHLY/YEARLY BASIS

HOW QUICKLY WOULD REPLACEMENT REUSABLE BOTTLES PAY FOR THEMSELVES?

- If a plastic bottle costs 50p for 500 ml and a reusable water bottle costs £15, you would have to use the reusable bottle 30 times to pay off the cost, but from that moment on you save 50p every time you fill up.
- If you avoided buying two plastic water bottles a week for a whole school year you would save £39!

STEP 2 – FIND AN ALTERNATIVE

- Research different companies that make and sell reusable bottles, prioritizing those based in the country where you live.

CREATE A LIST OF THE TOP 5 WITH THEIR CONTACT DETAILS

1.

2.

3.

4.

5.

- Work out how many bottles you would need in order to provide one for every student in your school and draft an email asking each company how much it would cost to buy that number of bottles.

- Once you have two or more different prices from companies, send a letter to your head teacher asking if the school would consider buying the bottles and explaining your calculations from Step 1. Focus on why this is important for the environment, but also how it could save money for the school by reducing clean-up costs.

- If the school is unable to cover the cost of purchasing bottles, then think about a way to raise money for the project (see page 198 in the 'Tips and Tricks' chapter).

STEP 3 – PLAN THE ROLL-OUT

- Speak to the school about banning single-use plastic bottles on site; this will make it easier to introduce the reusable bottles.

- Make sure there are enough drinking water taps or refill stations in the school. If there aren't, then think about how to convince the school to install more (see Step 5 below).

- To convince the school this project will work financially, suggest a scheme where students pay a small deposit for their reusable bottle. This would cover the cost of a replacement if the bottle is damaged or lost. Ensure the school is happy to keep a record of who has paid a deposit and hold the money.

- Speak to the school about printing the school logo on the bottles or creating sustainable stickers to hand out to students.

STEP 4 – DELIVER

- Once the bottles have been bought, arrange an assembly to introduce your scheme to other students and explain why cutting down on single-use plastic is important.

- Review progress after a month and conduct another series of litter picks on your school grounds to compare the results to your initial survey.

STEP 5 – NEXT STEPS

- Share the progress with everyone through the school newsletter and website.
- Think about how you can build on your success, for instance by using Action 17 on page 100 to research all the single-use plastic items your school uses, from pens to food packaging and cutlery, and start a campaign to exchange these for alternatives using the campaign guide on page 152.
- Use your success to set up a school eco-club and inspire more students to join you in taking environmental action, and share your approach with other schools (see Action 21 on page 125).

WHAT WILL IT ACHIEVE?

If your school has 1,000 students and they were all using a reusable bottle for a school year and no longer buying a single-use plastic bottle three times a week, then they would save 117,000 plastic bottles from ending up in the bin, nearly 19 tonnes of CO_2e and £58,500. Just think of the savings for people and the planet if everyone switched to a reusable bottle.

ORGANIZE AND CARRY OUT A CLEAN-UP EVENT
IN AN AREA OF GREEN SPACE

WHY?

- Over two million pieces of litter are dropped in the UK every day, from crisp packets to cigarettes, costing us £1 billion a year to clean up.

- Litter takes years to break down and can be harmful to people and wildlife, whether it is plastic microfibres in the air or harmful chemicals in our rivers.

We can turn the litter problem on its head and make it an opportunity to invest time and care in our communities and improve them together, while doing good for the planet at the same time.

WHAT YOU'LL NEED

PROTECTIVE GLOVES

RUBBISH AND RECYCLING BAGS

LITTER PICKERS

CONTAINER
FOR SHARP OR
HAZARDOUS
OBJECTS

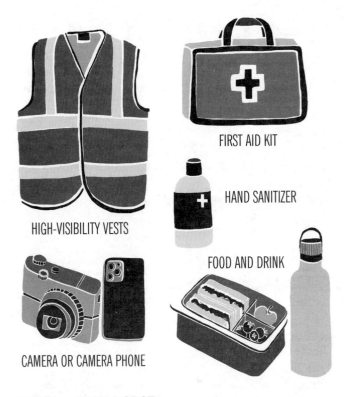

FIRST AID KIT

HAND SANITIZER

HIGH-VISIBILITY VESTS

FOOD AND DRINK

CAMERA OR CAMERA PHONE

STEP 1 – PICK A SPOT

- Look for areas where litter is a problem. This could be somewhere with high footfall (a large number of people using the area) or where people eat and drink outside.

- This can be a green space of some kind, but it doesn't have to be. Litter is a problem wherever it is, as it is blown by the wind into hedgerows and trees and washed into rivers and streams by the rain.

- Once you have identified a few possible sites, take your top pick and get permission to litter pick there (see page 191 in the 'Tips and Tricks' chapter for advice on how to get permission). Be prepared to try your back-up sites if you are unsuccessful.

STEP 2 – GET A GROUP TOGETHER

- Once you have found a spot it is time to get some help. Many hands make light work.

- There are plenty of organized litter clean-ups. The charity Keep Britain Tidy organizes the yearly Great British Spring Clean across the UK and has local volunteer groups led by #litterheroes.

- If there isn't a group in your area you could organize your own clean-up with Keep Britain Tidy through your school.

STEP 3 – PLAN YOUR CLEAN

- Decide on a date and time for your clean-up and ask an adult to supervise on the day.

- Think about what equipment you are going to need and work out where you can get it from (see page 188 in the 'Tips and Tricks' chapter for guidance). If you need to fundraise to cover the costs of equipment, use page 198 to help you do this.

- Check what materials your local council will recycle and make sure you have enough bags so that you can separate out recyclable materials on the day.

- Plan who will collect all of the rubbish at the end of the day. You can contact the local council, explain when you plan to do your clean-up and where and request that they remove rubbish.

- If you are planning to get more people involved, start advertising the date, timings, meeting location and what people need to bring.

- You could even think about a prize for those who collect the largest amount of rubbish.

STEP 4 – PICK UP THE PACE

- When the big day arrives, make sure you arrive nice and early to greet everyone joining you for the clean-up.

- Show people where they will be collecting rubbish, assign people to groups and specific locations if you have a large area and a lot of helpers, and explain how to separate out recyclable and non-recyclable material into the correct bags.

- Bring some hot or cold drinks, depending on the weather, and some snacks to keep everyone happy and hydrated during the day.

- Take some photos of the site before you begin the clean-up.

- Start the clean-up and watch and record with vlogs and photos as the site transforms through all your hard work.

- Make sure you record the number of bags of rubbish and recyclables you have collected and how many people volunteered.

- Take some photos of the site again once you've finished, or create a time-lapse video showing the whole clean-up.

STEP 5 – NEXT STEPS

- Your school group can submit your records from your clean-up to Keep Britain Tidy through their 'Dashboard' page.

- Think about organizing an even bigger clean-up with more members of your community for the Great British Spring Clean.

- Use clean, safe rubbish you collected to create a sculpture and showcase it in your school, local community centre or library with an explanation of where the rubbish has come from.

- Use the data you have collected to persuade decision-makers to install more rubbish and recycling bins at the site using Action 31 on page 174.

- Remember, litter picking is something you can do at any time wherever you are. See a piece of litter, pick it up and put it in a bin – it is a mindset and a responsible and caring approach to being outside and looking after the environment.

WHAT WILL IT ACHIEVE?

By organizing a clean-up, you are directly and positively impacting wildlife and your local community. While it may feel like a big challenge, you are now part of a growing movement of people who want to do more for the places where they live and the wildlife that shares these spaces.

LOCATION & DATE OF CLEAN-UP

LENGTH OF CLEAN-UP IN MINUTES

NUMBER OF VOLUNTEERS WHO TOOK PART

NUMBER OF BAGS OF RUBBISH COLLECTED

NUMBER OF BAGS OF PLASTIC BOTTLES COLLECTED

NUMBER OF BAGS OF ALUMINIUM CANS COLLECTED

LIST OF TOP 5 MOST COMMON ITEMS

ANY SURPRISE ITEMS?

ACTION 20 — RIPPLE EFFECT

HOW TO CLEAN UP AND PREVENT RIVER AND OCEAN POLLUTION

WHY?

- Three-quarters of England's rivers fail to meet healthy environmental standards. The threats facing rivers around the world are huge, and include climate breakdown, pollution and drainage from farming.

- Around 5,000 pieces of plastic pollution, including 150 plastic bottles, have been found per mile of beach in the UK, and plastic pollution has been found on every coastline in the world.

We can do more to keep our rivers and beaches clean, and it can start right now!

WHAT YOU'LL NEED

RUBBISH AND RECYCLING BAGS

PROTECTIVE GLOVES

LITTER PICKERS

CONTAINER FOR SHARP OR HAZARDOUS OBJECTS

HIGH-VISIBILITY VESTS

FIRST AID KIT

HAND SANITIZER

CAMERA OR CAMERA PHONE

FOOD AND DRINK

WATERPROOF CLOTHING

PEN AND PAPER OR NOTEBOOK

STEP 1 – FIND A RIVER OR BEACH

- Look at nearby rivers or beaches and identify one that is suffering from a litter problem.

- The Rivers Trust have lots of fantastic resources on UK rivers, including an interactive map where you can look at water quality and the causes of pollution in rivers near you – look for 'How healthy is your river?'.

IMPORTANT

Never enter a stream or river without responsible adults with you who know the area and have entered the river before. There can be dangerous currents in rivers and they can behave unpredictably. Never enter the sea during a beach clean. This can be a risk to life.

STEP 2 – JOIN A CLEAN-UP OR START YOUR OWN

- Once you have identified your spot, it is time to find a local group to help with your clean-up and to make sure you do this safely.

- The UK Rivers Network has a helpful list of local and national groups and the National Trust and Surfers Against Sewage organize regular beach cleans.

- If there isn't a clean-up event near you then you could set one up yourself. Surfers Against Sewage have a helpful guide to setting up a successful beach clean with your school and you can contact a local river group via the UK Rivers Network and ask for help too.

- Recruit your friends and family to join you on a clean-up or to help you to start a new one.

STEP 3 – GET IN THE FLOW

- If you are working with an organization, they should be able to provide the equipment you need.
- Dress up warmly and take plenty of food and hot drinks with you.
- At the end of your first clean-up, record what you have collected and the amount and then share the information with everyone involved.
- Make sure to organize another clean-up after some time has passed to see how much litter there still is in the river or on the beach.

STEP 4 – NEXT STEPS

- Turn your attention to solving the cause of the problem with a campaign to reduce pollution (see Action 32 on page 176).

WHAT WILL IT ACHIEVE?

Rivers and streams can recover quickly if we clean them up, and with the twelfth-longest coastline of any country in the world, there are plenty of beaches to investigate in the UK. By taking action you will have had a very real and positive impact on wildlife. More importantly, you will be setting an example to others.

INTRODUCTION

People in power should be held to account and the only way we can do this is to challenge them on the things that need changing and make sure they hear our concerns. There are a number of ways to share your voice and work with other people to bring about change. Whether you write a letter to a decision-maker, set up an eco-club with other young people or attend a peaceful protest, don't be afraid to speak your mind. Speak out, speak up and speak often.

'You often feel like the only person who cares about nature – you need to know that there are other people like you who care.'

DEEP SHAH

PHOTO © ACTION FOR CONSERVATION

The wind blew across the surface of the wide lake; miniature waves lapped at the base of the trees on the bank. Over the top of the highest branches, Deep Shah could see rolling green hills. Deep was 13 when his family took him to the Lake District. It was the first time he had left the city to visit one of the UK's national parks. It felt wild and exciting. He had never seen anything like it.

Back home, Deep thought often of what he had seen and the awe he had felt. The negative news coverage about the environment caught his attention more and more. It sparked something in him that hadn't existed before. He felt heartbroken to see species going extinct and people losing their lives and livelihoods as a result of climate breakdown. Overwhelmed by the scale of the problem, he kept thinking, 'what will I say to future generations if I don't act now?' No one at school seemed to be talking about these issues and so he applied to join an Action for Conservation residential camp with other young people interested in the environment to learn more. This time he visited the Pembrokeshire Coast National Park. As well as taking in the beauty all around him, he learnt that there is a lot missing from this landscape: species that have been lost. He was determined to find ways to bring wildlife back.

Deep changed his own lifestyle first. He switched to organic food, started taking shorter showers, travelled only by public transport and always recycled. Then he turned his attention to people close to him, like his family and neighbours. They didn't care about the environment as much as he thought they would, but he worked hard to understand why and change their views, suggesting changes they could make to their lifestyles that would add up to a big impact.

Next he started a school environmental society with a friend. They spoke to a teacher, got permission and started arranging meetings every week. They decided to organize a plastic bottle recycling project. A clever reward system – queue-jump cards for the school canteen – pulled in people who weren't originally interested in recycling. They made plans to create wildlife habitats around the school, plant wild flowers, build bird feeders and engage more of their fellow students in the process.

As the group grew, Deep felt motivated by other young people taking action with him. It reinforced his desire to drive change and convince even more people. He began to feel part of something bigger, a sense of solidarity. He decided to find other ways to make his voice heard. He joined his first protest and chanted out for all the plants and animals that have no voice. He wrote articles for different magazines about climate breakdown and how we should balance the needs of people and nature, and joined a ground-breaking, large-scale nature restoration project led by young people in Wales.

Focusing his sights on nature back home, Deep continued to fight for the environment. Near where he lives there is a large area of old military land. Its woodland and scrub have become a safe haven for wildlife in the city. The land went up for sale and it looked like a property developer would purchase and build on it, destroying this valuable habitat in the process. Deep decided to write to his local Member of Parliament (MP) about it. He carefully set out his arguments about the value of the area for people and wildlife. Eventually the MP wrote back and said he would be doing all he could to prevent the sale from going ahead. Success. Until the political winds changed direction following the general election. Now Deep has a new MP and the sale looks like it will be going ahead. Time to write his next letter!

DEEP'S MESSAGE TO YOU

It doesn't matter how small an act is, it will still have a bigger impact than doing nothing. You often feel like the only person who cares about nature – you need to know that there are other people like you who care. A great way to feel part of a group is to join or even form an environmental group in your local area or your school. With more people you can do more.

ACTION 21   FIND A CREW

START A SCHOOL ECO-CLUB LIKE DEEP!

WHY?

- There is no better feeling than having a close group of people who care about the same issues and who can use their different strengths and skills, support each other and create change together on a bigger scale.

- Never underestimate the power of a team! You can do more together.

STEP 1 – RECRUIT A GROUP AND DECIDE ON YOUR PURPOSE

- Advertise your club in your school newsletter and on your school website.

- Remember, you can have a club with as little as three people!

- Organize an informal first meeting to discuss what you want to do as a group – your purpose. This could be things like running campaigns or taking practical action for wildlife.

- Decide what kind of group you want to be and explore which issues you want to tackle.

- Decide on specific roles for members of your group, like Head of Research or Head of Fundraising. These roles could rotate around the group.

STEP 2 – GET PERMISSION AND FIND A PLACE TO MEET

- Ask your head teacher for permission to form as an official group. Explain that you want to help the school actively tackle the environmental crisis.

- Find somewhere that you can meet regularly, like a classroom after school or during lunch break.

- Seek support from your Science or Geography teachers, or your tutor.

STEP 3 – PROVE WHAT YOU CAN DO

- Your club could deliver any actions in this book and more. Doing it together will make it happen faster than if you were taking action alone.

- Start with small, easily achievable projects first to get warmed up and work out how your group works best together.

- Next, start to do bigger and more high-profile projects so that other students know that your group exists and join you.

STEP 4 – NEXT STEPS

- Once you are up and running start reaching out to other schools, like Esther. Write to their head teachers and ask whether they have an eco-club or society. If they do, ask to be put in touch with them and if they don't, offer to help the school set one up using your experience.

- Speak to your school about organizing an inter-school eco-club meeting. You could host this at your school or at a community centre. Invite members of eco-clubs and teachers at all the schools in your area and use it as an opportunity to share what you are already doing.

- Make it a regular thing and meet every few months. You could start planning an inter-school project and combine the energy, inspiration and passion of all your clubs into a super-team that achieves great things in your local area. Once you have this many young people on board and leading change, the sky is the limit.

SPEAK TRUTH TO THOSE IN POWER

HOW TO WRITE TO POLITICIANS OR OTHER LOCAL DECISION-MAKERS

Sometimes you might need to contact someone in a position of power to help you in your fight for change or to convince them to change how they are doing things. Here is how to contact them by email or letter.

STEP 1 – STRUCTURE YOUR LETTER OR EMAIL

 TIP

The letter can be adapted into an email by removing the address formatting at the top.

Your Name

Full Address

Postcode

Email/Other Contact Details

Name of the Person You Are Writing to

Their Address

Date

Dear [Mr/Mrs/Miss/Ms/Mx and person's surname or title if they have one]

Subject of your letter in bold (one line explaining your letter). If you are writing an email then this can go in the email subject line rather than here.

Paragraph 1

• Introduce who you are, where you are from and mention any groups you are already involved in.

 In the case of writing to a politician, it is best if you are in their constituency.

• Explain why you are contacting them – describe the issue.

• Discuss why this is an important issue and why they should be concerned about it – talk about the impacts locally and how this contributes to global issues too (use some facts and figures here).

Paragraph 2

• Talk about your ideas for possible solutions to this problem and how you think they might work.

• Explain that you would be interested in helping make these solutions a reality with their help.

Paragraph 3

• Explain why you are writing to them specifically and how you think they can help.

 It is important to be as clear as possible with what you would like them to do. It will be harder for them to ignore this if you are specific.

• Make sure to flatter them by researching something positive they have already done and saying how impressed you have been with it. If this links to the issue you are writing to them about, then even better.

Thank you for taking the time to consider my letter/email.
I look forward to hearing from you.

With best wishes,

Your Full Name

STEP 2 – SEND!

- Once you have drafted your letter, ask an adult to read through it. Pick someone who knows nothing about the issue you are writing about – if what you have written is clear to them, then it should make sense to the person you are writing to.

- Make sure to do a final spell check and ensure the request for help is clear and specific.

- If you are sending a letter by post then make sure to include a return address on the envelope as well as in the letter itself, so that they can reply. You can find contact details for all UK MPs online.

STEP 3 – NEXT STEPS

- If you don't get a response immediately, don't give up. If you think it has been too long, write a short follow-up letter/email mentioning your first one. Still no response? Keep sending letters/emails until you do. Chances are they will respond before you get sick of it!

- You can put pressure on people to respond in other ways, including through protests, by mentioning your letter on social media and tagging the person in question, or their office/company account, or even attending an MP's 'surgery' to meet with them in person.

WHAT WILL IT ACHIEVE?

Our elected leaders and those in charge of businesses and other organizations that have an impact on the natural world should be accountable to us and act in the best interests of the people and the planet, rather than just pursuing profit or further power. By sending them a message you are making them accountable and exercising your right to be heard.

ACTION 23 FIND A PROTEST

HOW TO TAKE PART IN A PEACEFUL PROTEST SAFELY

WHY?

- A peaceful protest is any act or statement that demonstrates disapproval without the use of violence, including boycotts, petitions and protest marches.

- Peaceful protest is not for everyone, but it can be a fantastic way to make your voice louder and be heard by those in power.

- Protests are an act of hope and a way to feel a sense of solidarity with other people who share your concerns and want change like you do.

Drive change through peaceful but forceful means!

STEP 1 – FIND A PROTEST

- Search local groups and campaigning organizations online and sign up to newsletters to stay up to date with which marches are taking place. The UK Student Climate Network (UKSCN), which organizes the Fridays For Future youth strike for climate in the UK, lists upcoming strikes on their website.

 TIP Make sure your parent or guardian is aware of any contact you have with organizations on the internet.

STEP 2 – GET PERMISSION

- It's very important to discuss the idea of attending a protest with your parent or guardian and explain why you feel this is an important thing for you to do. You'll need to have their permission and support.

- Your parent or guardian may have certain concerns about you attending a peaceful protest, so think about what these might be in advance.
- Have an honest conversation with them about their concerns so that they feel they have been heard and you are able to reach an agreement. Look at the UKSCN Adult Allies guide for extra help.

REMEMBER

If you are going to be missing school then you and your parents or guardians will need to get consent from school in order for your absence to be legal. Use template letters provided by UKSCN or draft your own letter.

STEP 3 – PREPARE FOR THE DAY

- Create a banner or placard. You can use a large piece of card and write your eye-catching message or slogan or dig out some paints and get creative.
- Familiarize yourself with the protest location or route of the march. If possible, visit beforehand.
- Always attend a protest with at least one person you know and stick together – it is more fun and safer this way. Make sure you arrange a meeting point within view of the protest in a public place and an agreed time towards the end of the planned protest in case you lose each other in the crowd or your phone runs out of battery or service.
- Spread the word about the protest online and in person among friends before you go.
- Carefully plan your travel for the day. For some protests, organizers will ensure there are buses running to enable those living further away to attend, but this won't always be the case. Aim to use public transport if you can, but check for any route or service closures on protest day, especially in the area around the protest.

STEP 4 – ON THE DAY

Things to take on the day:

• A fully charged phone and a portable battery if you have one.

• Refillable water bottle.

• A whistle.

• Food – you don't want to run out!

• Some money for any unexpected costs.

• Depending on the time of year and weather – a rain jacket and extra warm clothes, including jumper, hat (for sun or cold!) and gloves.

• A small backpack to carry everything in.

• Your banner or placard.

• Passion and a loud voice.

Leave plenty of time to get to the meeting point on the day. Have fun!

WHAT WILL IT ACHIEVE?

Peaceful protest has been a part of most of the big social movements we have seen in human history, from the abolition of slavery to Black Lives Matter, and from women's suffrage to LGBTQ+ rights. The environmental crisis is one of the greatest threats facing humanity and the planet. By joining peaceful protests, you are participating in an act of hope in solidarity with millions of other heroes across the world, and you are placing yourself on the right side of history.

'We need to
preserve this
precious connection
to nature that
we have.'
DARA MCANULTY

PHOTO © ELAINE HILL

Dara McAnulty held the worm in the palm of his hand. It
wriggled for a few seconds and then went quite still. He
counted the rings around its body carefully before putting
it back on the earth. He found earthworms fascinating. He
loved finding bird feathers too. At first, he couldn't understand
why other children at his primary school in Belfast weren't as
interested in the feathers he had collected. He soon realized he
was different.

Dara is autistic. It means he sees the world more intensely
and he notices things other people wouldn't. Colours can flash
across his vision as his emotions intensify. It has given him
a deep connection to nature and the species we share the
planet with. But the world can also feel overwhelming at times,
particularly when he is away from green places.

At school, some of the other children would bully him for
being so passionate about the natural world. He felt isolated
and lonely. He had to find a way to escape them and to talk
about the inspiring things he would see all around him. So, at
the age of 12, Dara decided to start a blog about nature. He
loved words and enjoyed organizing his thoughts on the page.
The blog gave him an opportunity to research the things he

saw around him and record his experiences. With each new landscape and blog post he would learn a little more, which would subtly change the way he wrote. He started to write poetry too – another way to pin his emotions to the page with words.

Dara wrote for himself. He didn't know if anyone else was reading his blog. Then a few comments started to appear. Before long, people were commenting on all his posts. His following grew and grew. He joined social media and started communicating with a much bigger community of people who care about nature. It was reassuring to discover all these people. He wasn't alone, and he realized he could ignore the bullies. It was their problem, not his.

Then an amazing thing happened: an independent publisher of nature writing got in touch to discuss putting Dara's blog posts together into a book. Before he knew it, at the age of 14, Dara was writing a book about how autism and his experiences of nature have affected his life. He wrote about what was going on in his head and in the world around him with each passing season over a whole year. He called it the *Diary of a Young Naturalist*. Dara felt a mixture of emotions as he opened himself up and poured everything on to the page. Reliving the bullying was hard, but the writing helped him understand and come to terms with what had happened. The book gave him a way to make sense of it all. Now other young people can read his story too.

DARA'S MESSAGE TO YOU

Notice the world, see the creatures and the world becomes so much wider, stranger and more beautiful. If everyone could view the world as this impossibly big and connected ecosystem, the world would be a better place. We need to preserve this precious connection to nature that we have.

WRITE THE CHANGE

WRITE AN ARTICLE FOR A LOCAL NEWSPAPER OR MAGAZINE,
A BLOG POST OR TEXT FOR A WEBSITE

- -

WHY?

- To be an effective environmentalist it helps to be able to communicate with other people.

- There are many creative ways to communicate, and writing is just one of them. If you prefer art, film, theatre or music that is great – use your skills, it will make it more fun.

STEP 1 – DECIDE WHAT YOU WANT TO WRITE ABOUT AND WHERE

- Decide where your work will feature: is it a blog (your own one or someone else's), is it for a local newspaper or magazine, for a website or something else? Whichever it is, spend some time looking at other similar articles and make some notes on the normal length, style of the writing and who you think might be a typical reader and what they might want to hear about. Check whether they have any specific writing guidelines for submitting an article.

- You can write about anything you like – it doesn't matter if it is greenhouse gas emissions, green caterpillars or green businesses.

- Keep your subject focused for your first piece; you can always write about broader subjects in future. Use personal experiences as these can make your piece more exciting and engaging and it is easier to write about things you know or have done yourself.

STEP 2 – MAKE A PLAN

- Using your notes on style, length and with your reader in mind, start to plan your piece of writing.

- You can create headings to help you get started and write some short bullet points detailing what kind of things you want to say for each section.

- The introduction should briefly tell the story of the whole piece in a way that is engaging and encourages the reader to read on. You can pose a few unanswered questions to make it intriguing. For example, if you were writing a piece about a new nature site that you have created in your school grounds, you would want to give a quick overview of what you have done with a few catchy facts about wildlife, and then ask why the reader might think it is important. You can then explain why in your article.

- The main body of the text is where you can let your storytelling come to life. Ideally you want a logical set of points that form a narrative (a story), across several paragraphs.

- With each new paragraph introduce something new to the reader, such as a different viewpoint or additional piece of information. Using the example of a nature site, your first paragraph might focus on the risks facing wildlife in the UK, the second paragraph might talk about possible solutions to the problem and the third paragraph might talk about your solution (the new nature site) and how you will monitor progress.

- The conclusion should bring everything to a clear end, whatever that end is, and refer back to the original focus of the article.

- It is good to end with a final sentence that provokes further reflection from the reader, leaves certain questions unanswered or encourages them to take action.

STEP 3 – DRAFT IT

- Draft your piece of writing. There is no set way to write. You will develop your own approach over time and with practice, but if you are new to this try starting at the beginning, with the introduction, and then work your way through!

- Once you have written your conclusion, go back to the introduction. It will usually need some rewriting at this stage.

- Review your main paragraphs and your conclusion and rewrite as necessary. Ask yourself if the points are clear, whether you are saying what you want to say, if you are providing an accurate impression, if the story is captivating and if you have the right evidence to back up your points.

- Keep editing and make it as clear and concise as possible, cutting out unnecessary words and making sentences short and attention-grabbing. Expect to cut it by as much as 50% during this editing process.

- Check for spelling mistakes and grammatical errors and make adjustments until you have a final draft.

WRITING TIPS:

- Use facts and figures, but try to fit these within your story rather than just list lots of facts.
- Include quotes from people you have interviewed or take quotes from other articles, books, television or film. Characters, whether people, plants or animals, can bring your story to life and draw your reader in.

STEP 4 – PERFECT AND PITCH

- Create a catchy title that grabs the reader's attention.

- Send the draft to someone you trust and ask them to review it and suggest edits or corrections. It is helpful to have someone who doesn't know about the content of your article review it with a fresh pair of eyes.

- Ask for honest feedback and consider it carefully.

- In the end, it is up to you what advice you take on board and what you ignore. Keep in mind your original notes about where you aim to publish the article and who your readers will be.

- Send an email to the editor of your target blog, website, newspaper or magazine explaining in two concise but attention-grabbing sentences what your article is about and asking the editor to publish it.

- Include some photos with your writing if you have permission to use them.

- If you get a negative response from your first choice then approach some other options. You might need to make a few edits so that it is suitable and meets any new writing guidelines or their publication style.

- Some writing won't get published. This is completely normal. Don't feel disappointed and don't stop writing. It is never a waste of your time; in fact, it is incredibly useful experience, will expand your knowledge and it means that your next piece will be even better.

- Create your own blog so that you can post all your articles on it (whether or not they get published elsewhere). This will act as a catalogue of all your work! You never know, like Dara, you might end up having a book published.

STEP 5 – NEXT STEPS

- Write another piece . . . and another. Get loud with your pen or your keyboard. Exercise that muscle and get your voice out there and share your opinions and perspectives.

- Explore other ways to share your voice, like recording a podcast, creating a vlog, film or animation, drawing a comic strip, building a website, writing a song or a play, or making a piece of art using recycled materials to raise awareness about an issue you care about.

WHAT WILL IT ACHIEVE?

Stories can change the world, so start telling yours and tell it often. If just one person sees something from a different perspective or changes their behaviour as a result of something you have written, then you have had an amazing impact and already created a legacy in this world.

MAKE IT RELEVANT

APPROACH A LOCAL CONSERVATION ORGANIZATION AND ASK TO
HELP IMPROVE INFORMATION BOARDS IN A PARK OR NATURE
RESERVE TO APPEAL TO OTHER YOUNG PEOPLE YOUR AGE

WHY?

- Information on education boards in our wildlife areas is
  often out of date, old-fashioned or just plain boring.

- Changing the way people engage with information in our
  wildlife areas and making the content fresh and interesting
  can make green spaces and wildlife more attractive and
  relevant to younger generations.

- Who better to improve the way in which we communicate
  information in our wildlife areas than creative young people
  like you? It is time to get designing!

STEP 1 – IDENTIFY A GREEN SPACE

- Find a local green space with a lack of information about
  the wildlife or work going on to protect it or information
  boards that aren't engaging for someone your age.

- Identify who manages or owns the area. This may be
  obvious from signs that are there or you may need to do
  some research online.

- Draft an email or letter and introduce yourself (see Action
  22 on page 127 for help). Explain politely that you enjoy
  visiting the area and have ideas for how to make the
  information boards more engaging for young people in
  particular. Ask to meet with them to discuss whether and
  how you might be able to collaborate with them to do this.

- If you get a negative response you could try again or look
  at a different wildlife area – once you have successfully
  started a project elsewhere, the organization managing
  the original site might take notice and be more open to
  discussing your ideas.

STEP 2 – COME UP WITH YOUR DESIGNS

- Come up with two or three different designs to take to the meeting.

- You could draw designs for new information boards using the existing information, or design completely new boards with new information on local species, environmental issues and solutions.

- Think about the language, pictures and style that will be most engaging to your generation – ask yourself what you like and get your friends to comment and give you some ideas.

- You don't need to have a lot of detailed information at this stage – you just want to do enough to give an idea of what you are thinking about.

- Identify what materials you could use to make the new signs and information boards more sustainable.

- Physical boards go out of date quickly, so explore ways to make them more easily updatable, such as reusable, replaceable panels or even screens that can be updated with new information more regularly.

- You could suggest digital solutions, such as QR codes for people to scan with their smart phones to access more detailed information, or even some kind of app-based wildlife trail. This would have the benefit of reducing the visual impact of physical information boards in a beautiful wildlife area.

STEP 3 – AGREE ON THE RIGHT DESIGN

- Present your designs and ideas. You might come up against challenges, such as a lack of funds or needing further approval from a board of trustees or local council.

- Offer to help fundraise for the project if they don't have enough money (see page 198 in the 'Tips and Tricks' chapter).

- If they are willing to move forward, decide on the process for creating the information boards together with members of the organization. You could involve other young people, like friends or members of your school eco-club.

STEP 4 – INSTALL AND LAUNCH

- Plan a launch event. You could include food stalls and competitions, such as a wildlife scavenger hunt, and invite local celebrities and the press for maximum publicity.

- Invite local families through community groups and school groups and publicize the launch in local newspapers (see page 201 in the 'Tips and Tricks' chapter).

STEP 5 – NEXT STEPS

- If you have success in one area, extend your approach to other areas nearby.

- Speak to your school about linking your new information boards with your school's curriculum and using green space as a location for regular outdoor learning sessions (see Action 3 on page 13).

- Organize wildlife walks which include stops at your information boards using Action 7 on page 42.

WHAT WILL IT ACHIEVE?

Engaging other young people in the nature on their doorstep is a critical step towards building a society that cares about wildlife and wants to live in harmony with it. By helping organizations work to better engage young people, you are providing an incredible service to your community and all life in it!

PRINCESS'S STORY

'Try out new things and don't be afraid to fail. You will find out what is right for you by getting things wrong.'

PRINCESS-JOY EMEANUWA

PHOTO © PRINCESS-JOY EMEANUWA

Princess-Joy Emeanuwa could see her dad through the window, kneeling next to his plants, whispering. Her father liked to grow his own food in their garden in South London; it reminded him of his childhood in Nigeria. Sometimes he would talk to his plants to help them grow. The garden was teeming with life. Seeing her father's love and respect for his plants inspired Princess to feel the same.

In her second year of secondary school, she met someone who would help her use that respect to help nature. Mr Davis was Princess's Geography teacher. He organized a group of students to pick up litter in the River Cray with the support of a charity called Thames21. Princess enjoyed learning about the environment while she did something practical to help it and decided she would keep coming back to the River Cray. Mr Davis suggested she enter a competition for a place on an environmental camp.

Princess loved the opportunity to visit the countryside for the first time and learn about how she could make a difference where she lived. She felt exhausted on the train home after the camp – her brain was whirring with everything she had seen, heard and done and ideas for actions she could take once she got home.

Back in the city, she started to make her voice heard on the different issues that were important to her. Princess and her friends wanted young people to have a say in the government's decisions about the environment. The timing was just right. The government was developing the Environment Bill, a set of new proposals on the environment and its protection, and environmental organizations were gathering thousands of people in front of the Houses of Parliament to talk about the key issues at a Mass Lobby. Princess and her friends developed a manifesto for change, and presented it to MPs and over three hundred young people at the Mass Lobby. It felt good to talk about their ideas, but it was hard to be heard above all the noise and commotion. Princess had another idea. She knew that some government officials would be visiting her school a month later to talk to teachers. She printed off copies of the manifesto, walked straight up and gave it to them. She asked them to give the manifesto to the team working on the Environment Bill. Princess is now in touch with the right people; they have seen the manifesto and Princess is hoping to organize a meeting to discuss how they can work with young people in the future.

As Princess has learnt more, she has gained confidence and discovered a love of public speaking. She felt honoured and a little scared to be asked to talk at the launch event for London as a National Park City, where she would share the stage with the Mayor. When the day arrived, the audience at City Hall was packed with people. Princess felt nervous, her heart was beating fast and butterflies danced in her stomach. Soon it was her turn to speak. Though she was nervous she knew she just needed to tell it how it is. As she spoke the words poured out of her mouth, like butterflies fluttering up towards the light. Members of the audience began to smile and nod. People actually care about my opinion, she thought. She felt amazing, like she could do anything.

Princess has continued to find ways to make her voice heard for nature. She became a Trustee for Action for Conservation. In this role she has been able to contribute her experience and improve how the charity inspires and empowers young people to take action for nature. She joined the Penpont Project, the world's largest youth-led nature restoration initiative, where she hopes to pioneer new approaches to saving wildlife with other young people. Next she wants to change the education system. Princess thinks volunteering for the environment could form part of the curriculum. She is making her dad proud.

PRINCESS'S MESSAGE TO YOU

I have been inspired by the many young people taking action on the issues we all care about. The momentum behind our voice is powerful, so never be afraid to use yours! You can make a change where you live, whether it's by growing a garden on your balcony or volunteering in your community's blue and green spaces. Remember, you don't have to be an expert to know something is wrong and do something about it. I am an environmentalist because these issues affect our quality of life, from health and education to food and transport. Explore what interests you about the environment. Try out new things and don't be afraid to fail. You will find out what is right for you by getting things wrong.

FIND YOUR PLACE

APPLY FOR YOUTH DECISION-MAKING POSITIONS, AND IF
THEY DON'T EXIST, CREATE THEM

WHY?

* Young people are poorly represented when it comes to
  decisions made about a range of social and environmental
  issues. For example, less than 3% of charity trustees, the
  people with ultimate responsibility for running charities,
  are under 30.

* Young people's voices are important, especially with
  intergenerational issues like extinction and climate
  breakdown. Decisions made now will affect young people
  in the future.

A great way for you to have a voice is to join Princess and apply
for positions on decision-making bodies, such as youth advisory
panels or committees in charities, businesses, community
groups and schools. If such positions don't exist, then you can
push for their creation.

STEP 1 – FIND AN OPPORTUNITY OR ORGANIZATION

* Search online for organizations that interest you, sign up
  to newsletters and look out for opportunities.

* Speak to your school and local community groups and
  contact your council and tell them that you are interested
  in youth positions on advisory boards or committees in case
  they hear of any.

STEP 2 – APPLY

* Watch out for age limitations – in order to become a full
  trustee of a charity in the UK you will most likely have to
  be 18 or in some cases 16.

- Be creative and original – if there is no set format why not send in a video explaining why you would be a good fit for the role.

- Show what you know – make sure you understand the organization you are applying to, what issues they tackle and why and how they do it.

- Explain what you can bring – the organization won't expect you to be an expert. You bring the perspectives of your generation into their planning and how they can communicate better with your generation and involve you in their work.

- If there don't seem to be opportunities for young people to get involved in an organization you want to get involved in, then contact them and push to create some (see Action 22 on page 127 for advice on drafting an email or letter).

IF YOU EMAIL AN ORGANIZATION TO SUGGEST THEY CREATE A YOUTH ROLE, INCLUDE THE FOLLOWING:

- Who you are, how old you are and why you are interested in their work.
- Why you think it is important for young people to be involved in the work that they do.
- Explain that you have an interest in learning about how the organization is run and in helping them engage young people as supporters/volunteers.
- Ask if they would consider discussing the idea of trialling some youth involvement in decision-making with you.

TIP

Before you email, find out who runs the organization. Check its website for their name and contact details or those of someone else senior in the organization.

STEP 3 – GETTING STARTED

- This is an exciting opportunity to create change on a larger scale and learn new skills and the experience can benefit your studies and career in the long term.

- Read up on your responsibilities so that you are fully informed of your role.

- Make time before meetings to prepare your points and understand the issues at hand.

- Speak up and remember, there are no stupid questions.

STEP 4 – KEEP GROWING

- Few organizations will have a perfect model for engaging young people in decision-making. By joining them, you are helping them to better represent young people. It is important to be patient as everybody learns together.

- Come up with suggestions for how to improve things and keep things moving forward.

EXAMPLES OF IMPROVEMENTS:

- Change normal meeting times to ensure you don't miss school.

- Discuss complex areas like budgets before meetings with whoever is leading the meeting to ensure you understand.

- Change meeting formats to give young people time and space to speak.

- Have more than one youth representative to ensure your collective voice is stronger.

- Have a reporting mechanism so that ideas put forward by a youth panel are responded to by other decision-making bodies.

- Introduce job shadowing to allow you to understand different roles in the organization.

- Change the charitable structure of the organization to allow those aged 16 and over to become trustees.

- Don't let yourself be tokenized. Those running organizations have to make compromises and not everyone's ideas can be turned into action all of the time. But if at any point you feel you are just in the room for show or that people aren't respecting your opinions or responding to your ideas at all, then let them know how you feel. Explain why you are in the room and that you would like to create a plan for how you will be involved in decision-making in a more meaningful way. There are also organizations that can provide advice and support, such as the Young Trustees Movement.

- Once you have experience in one organization, you might want to develop your skills in another. It is helpful to leave an organization that has progressed well to join one that is at the beginning of its journey.

WHAT WILL IT ACHIEVE?

A big step towards making the future brighter for nature is to change the way current systems operate. Taking on a position in an existing organization, no matter what the size, is a chance to start changing things from the inside, with your future and that of other young people in mind.

CHAPTER 6 ENVIRONMENTAL CAMPAIGNS

INTRODUCTION

Now that you have delivered successful actions and feel confident using your voice, it might be time to take things to the next level and start an environmental campaign. Depending on where you are in the world, campaigning can sometimes be dangerous or difficult, so when setting up a campaign be aware of this and discuss it with your parents or guardians before you start.

If you have come to this chapter with an issue in mind already, then use the campaign guide to help you plan for success. If you are looking for inspiration then choose from the example campaigns, which will give you background information and ideas for actions and helpful tips, and then plan them out in more detail using the campaign guide.

CAMPAIGN GUIDE

STEP 1 – CREATE A CASE

- Research the issue you have identified and use the information you find to create a clear and compelling case for your campaign.

HOW TO STRUCTURE YOUR CASE

Make sure you keep sentences short and use clear language. Bullet points are a good idea to get the basic ideas across. You should also think about how you can make the information relevant to people.

- Part 1: Outline why you have come to care about this issue.
- Part 2: Talk about the impact this issue has on people and wildlife locally.
- Part 3: Explain how this issue links to global problems and give some facts to back this up.

- Next, list some solutions to the problem that you have identified, providing some detail about what you want people to do.

STEP 2 – IDENTIFY YOUR TARGET AND DECISION-MAKERS

- As you were developing your case, it will have become clear who your main target is for the campaign. This could be an organization, such as a school, business or community group, or an individual or group of individuals. For example, your target could be your school if you are trying to ban single-use plastic at school. It could also be fellow students if your aim is to increase recycling rates in your community.

- Where your target is an organization, try to narrow things down to the key decision-makers in that organization. In the example of the school above, it might be the head teacher. If it is a business it might be the chief executive, who runs the company.

- With large companies it is often hard to identify who the key decision-makers are so you can get in contact with them. Sometimes it might be better to start with a local 'grassroots' campaign to influence one branch of a business, for example an individual supermarket, and once this gets people's attention you could start to expand your campaign to the whole business.

STEP 3 – DECIDE ON YOUR AIM AND GOALS

- Focus your case into a main aim for your campaign. Make it nice and specific, for instance: to convince X supermarket to stock more packaging-free options.

- Identify 2–4 goals that will help you on your way to achieving this aim. For example:
  - Provide loose organic vegetable and fruit options.
  - Offer reusable bags for loose produce.
  - Trial a packaging-free refill station for dry goods.

Use the SMART framework to evaluate your aim
and goals:

- **Specific** – Do your campaign aim and goals address
  one particular issue? It is much better to have one
  real, small success than to try and change too many
  things at once, and not achieve anything!

- **Measurable** – Can you clearly check or measure
  whether your aim and goals have been met?

- **Achievable** – Your aim and goals should be
  ambitious, creative and exciting, but they will only
  lead to significant change if they are also achievable.

- **Relevant** – Choose an aim and goals that are
  relevant to who you are and what you care about.

- **Time-specific** – Do your aim and goals have
  particular end points and are they achievable within
  the time frame you have set yourself?

STEP 4 – THE SOFT START

- When you are dealing with a decision-maker in an
  organization, always start by asking directly for what you
  want before looking at other tactics. Use your case to draft
  a polite email or letter to the key decision-maker asking
  them for a meeting (see Action 22 on page 127 for
  a template).

- Meet with them to make the case in person, making sure
  to have a parent or guardian with you (see page 192 of the
  'Tips and Tricks' chapter for help). If they agree, identify
  a timeline for them to implement the change you are
  proposing.

- If they won't respond to your contact or they say no after
  meeting with you, then move to Step 5.

STEP 5 – PUT TOGETHER A CAMPAIGN TEAM

- Put together your campaign team. Speak to your friends and ask them to join you in your campaign (see page 193 in the 'Tips and Tricks' chapter for how to build a team).

STEP 6 – IDENTIFY YOUR AUDIENCE

- To be successful you need to encourage a larger number of people (your audience) to care about the issue you want to focus on and help you put pressure on your target.

- Your goals may be specific to certain groups of people or organizations, but it is good to think about all possible audiences.

- In some cases, your target will overlap with your audience. For example, if you are trying to get students at your school recycling, then the students are your target, but they are also going to be your audience.

- Start by writing your target or key decision-maker in the middle of a big piece of paper. Draw a circle round them. Next identify the different groups of people or organizations who could directly influence them and write these down around the circle. These are your different audiences.

- The following is an example list of audience categories. You will be able to think of others or adapt these to make them more relevant to your campaign:
  - Young people at your school
  - Young people at another school
  - Head teacher/teachers
  - Parents/guardians
  - Schools
  - Scientists
  - Student groups at universities or colleges
  - Campaigners/environmental charities
  - Local officials/local councils
  - Local business owners or businesses
  - Journalists or press
  - Tourists
- Use arrows to connect different audiences who might influence each other too. Wherever there is a connecting line make some notes about what kind of influence the group could have on each other and why.
- Create a colour key and code your audience: red = against your campaign aims; orange = neutral about your campaign aims; green = likely to support your campaign aims. Add the colours to every audience group on your map.
- Next, identify the motivations and key features of each group – this may be in general terms if you don't know them personally. This will help you identify what your audience members want and which arguments might persuade them to support your campaign.

AUDIENCE MOTIVATIONS

For a campaign about air pollution, take the example of a parent who owns a car but doesn't use it often:

- They are walking their children to school and running errands without using their car. This may indicate that they already have concerns about air pollution.

- They have children, and so if they are made aware of the risks they will care about the impact air pollution can have on their children in particular.

- They may spend time outside the school gates waiting to pick their children up, where idling engines cause a particularly large amount of air pollution, and this may be having an impact on their health (idling is where people leave engines running when they aren't driving).

- They have mild asthma and this seems to get worse when they are walking down the high street where there is usually bad traffic.

- If you can, try to identify one or more key motivations. In this case: their children's health and their own health.

STEP 7 – CAMPAIGN TACTICS

- Once you know who your target and audience are and what they care about, it is time to think about what tactics you will use.

- The best tactics will be those that encourage different audience groups to move from red to orange or orange to green, or that might encourage those you have coded as green to help influence your reds and oranges.

- It is often better to focus your time and effort on your orange audience groups first, as they will be easier to convince.

- Each time you come up with a tactic, ask yourself how this will appeal to people's motivations. What you do with one group might not work with others.

- Make sure that each tactic provides something specific and practical for people to do to help, like getting everyone to sign an online petition, join a community meeting, or write a letter to a politician or the council. Make sure the tactics highlight the things they care about.

- Here are some example tactics you can use:
  - Approach other organizations campaigning on this issue and join forces with them.
  - Draft a petition calling for one of your campaign goals to be implemented and collect signatures online using a petition-building website.
  - Get all your friends together and create fun flyers using recycled paper or use photography, art or vlogs to communicate about your campaign.
  - Spread the word at school by giving an assembly about your campaign, collect signatures for a petition or get students to write letters to your local council or a politician.
  - Contact your local newspaper and ask them to share your story or publicize any petitions you have created. Sometimes, just the threat that you will speak to the press is enough to drive change. Few organizations want to be seen to ignore a group of young people trying to do something good for the environment.
  - Write a letter to a politician or another public figure to ask for their support.
  - Hold an event, such as a concert, party or fundraiser, or organize a rally or march.
  - Turn up the heat and organize a boycott. To make this work you need to have enough people supporting your campaign, so make sure you assess the level of support before you start (the number of petition signatures could be a good indication).
- Always be clear about your aim and your goals when implementing your tactics, so that people understand why you are doing what you are doing. Use your campaign case as the basis for all your communications with different groups.
- Don't forget to collect contact details from everyone involved in the campaign and keep them informed of your progress. Once people are invested in the outcome, they will become more powerful allies.

STEP 8 – BE VICTORIOUS

- If a tactic doesn't work, evaluate why and adapt it accordingly. Perhaps there weren't enough people on your side, perhaps the message didn't get to the right people, perhaps it wasn't communicated in the right way.

- Remember, it is hard to convince other people to change their behaviour. Use the following section: 'Changing Hearts and Minds – Tips for Talking About the Environmental Crisis' and make sure your arguments are well researched and persuasive and that you are mindful of people's motivations and the pressures they face. Be compassionate, but uncompromising.

- Decision-makers may at some stage agree to meet you and offer you a compromise. It is up to you whether you feel their proposed steps go far enough or whether you need to keep pushing.

- Make sure you record the impact you have! As things improve this will convince others to join you; people like to be involved in what others around them are doing and enjoy being part of a success.

- Don't give up, and don't give in. Achieving your goal will have a direct and positive impact on people and nature.

- Remember to celebrate when you succeed with a tactic and to thank your target or decision-makers for making a positive change! You could hold an event to mark this special moment.

- If you achieve your goals more quickly than you expected then don't be afraid to stretch your aim and create new goals – there will be lots of ways you can achieve change.

CHANGING HEARTS AND MINDS
TIPS FOR TALKING ABOUT THE ENVIRONMENTAL CRISIS

- If people have different points of view from you, don't dismiss or mock them, even if you disagree with them. Try to understand their viewpoint, show respect and engage them in conversation. You can only change their minds if you can have a debate.

- Have a good opener. Start the conversation talking about something you have been reading about or are doing yourself.

- Avoid doom and gloom. Fear can cause people to switch off and the environmental crisis can definitely feel scary. Instead, talk about the opportunities: 'If we buy vegetables grown without the use of pesticides, we can avoid the harm these chemicals do to important insects like bees and eat food that is healthy for us' or 'If we take the train instead of driving we can read a book as we travel and do good for the environment at the same time'.

- Make it simple for them. Be ready with suggestions for how things can be done in a more environmentally friendly way.

- Talk about local effects to make it feel personal – highlight extreme weather events at home, such as more frequent and intense flooding or drought or the loss of a particular species or habitat nearby.

- Remember that people respond best to their peers and are more likely to do something other people around them are doing. So lead by example, and be the change that you want to see!

- Once you have had the first conversation, evaluate how it went. It is unlikely it will go exactly as planned, because what conversations do? In fact, it might feel like you didn't get anywhere first time around!

- Be patient, if you have been respectful and managed not to make the people angry or too defensive then you will have sown a seed with your first conversation.

- Focus on any reasons they gave for not changing their behaviour or taking action, and think about why they gave these reasons and what alternatives might exist. Come up with ways to respond to each.

- In some cases, there might not be an alternative or solution to a reason they gave. In this circumstance, your best approach in the next conversation is to openly acknowledge their reason and explain that you respect it, and then give some new reasons for why it is important to change.

- Over time you might begin to sense their position shifting. For some people this might happen quickly, perhaps over the course of just one conversation, for others it may take longer, and for some you might never be able to change their mind. This is OK – you can't succeed every time. What is important is that you keep trying and then you will succeed some of the time.

- At some point, they might say they are going to change the particular behaviour of their own accord or you might sense it is the right time to ask them to do it. If you do ask them, then ask respectfully. Don't make them feel like you told them so or give an impression that you are superior for having known this all along.

SOME CAMPAIGNS YOU CAN TRY . . .

ACTION 27 PLANE DRAIN

PERSUADING FAMILY AND FRIENDS THAT FLYING SHOULD
BE LEFT TO BIRDS

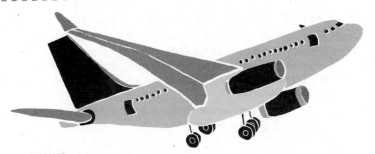

WHY?

- The carbon footprint of taking one long-haul flight (flying for seven hours or more) can be the same as driving a car for a year. Short-haul flights are often worse per mile travelled as more fuel is burnt during take-off and landing.

- Some long-haul flights might be unavoidable, but the majority of short-haul flights that are taken by a small percentage of people in society may not be necessary.

Recent events have led to a dramatic reduction in the number of flights people take, reducing this source of carbon emissions. We have a unique opportunity to convince people who used to be frequent flyers to cut down on flying, incentivizing the aviation industry and governments to come up with more green flight technologies and jobs instead.

CAMPAIGN TIPS

- Keep it simple. Look around and identify who has taken short-haul flights a lot in the past.

- You might find it takes a long time to convince someone you've identified to commit to taking fewer flights in the future, or it might be instant. You can also work to convince different people at the same time.

SHORT-HAUL, WHAT-HAUL?

- Short-haul flights are usually defined as flights that are up to three hours long or up to 700 miles in distance. Long-haul flights are usually defined as flights of seven hours or more, or around 2,400+ miles. Medium-haul flights are anywhere in between.

- Long-haul flights have a larger carbon footprint overall, but short-haul flights are much less efficient and have higher carbon emissions per mile.

- Use the Tips for Talking About the Environmental Crisis (on page 161) to work out how you are going to approach the subject with them, including having suggestions for alternative forms of travel prepared in advance.

- Once someone has expressed a commitment to not flying short-haul or at all, you should try to convince that person to pledge publicly not to fly in future alongside you and to discourage others from flying too.

- You can join a growing movement globally and pledge to the Flight Free campaign.

- As you start successfully convincing people not to fly in future, look further afield and start to convince people you know less well at school or in your local community.

WHAT WILL IT ACHIEVE?

There is no doubt that if people stop flying it can have a dramatic impact. A return flight from London to Hong Kong emits more carbon than eating meat or driving a car for a year and is equivalent to the production of 340,000 single-use plastic bags (and I don't think anyone is going to be using that many plastic bags in a lifetime). More importantly, by pledging not to fly we reduce future demand and put pressure on airlines and governments to clean up their act!

ACTION 28 ENOUGH ENGINES

SET UP A CAMPAIGN TO REDUCE CAR USE IN YOUR LOCAL AREA

WHY?

- Over 2,000 schools and other places of education are within 150 metres of roads with illegal levels of nitrogen dioxide, a pollutant that is harmful to our lungs.
- 36,000 deaths a year are linked to air pollution in the UK, and the figure rises to seven million worldwide.

But the good news is that more and more people are aware of the problem and are taking steps to reduce air pollution.

There are more sustainable forms of transport that are good for our health and the planet. Even making small changes to our existing modes of transport can have a dramatic, positive effect.

CAMPAIGN TIPS

- Explore the quality of air where you live. You can find UK data online on the National Atmospheric Emissions Inventory's interactive map.
- Make sure you are aware of existing laws around air quality. The charity ClientEarth provides lots of information.
- Work out where the biggest problem is locally, whether it is from school runs in cars, idling engines or high traffic areas.
- Decide on a specific campaign aim, such as: 'To reduce air pollution levels in three square miles around my school by X amount over the next two years'.

- Pick 2–4 goals that will help you achieve this aim that are SMART (see page 154) and that are appropriate for where you live. For example:
  - Get 50% of students cycling/walking to school more than three times a week within six months.
  - Submit a petition signed by 1,000 people asking the council to create new cycle lanes between, for example, a housing estate and a secondary school.
  - Convince 100 people to exchange their polluting car for public transport or a more efficient and less polluting hybrid or electric model.
- Once you are successful, you can always use your cutting-edge campaign skills and powers of persuasion to extend this approach elsewhere. Look at other areas locally; is there anywhere else where you could reduce air pollution?
- Share your approach with others by creating a toolkit for reducing air pollution or making available some of the campaign materials you have created.

WHAT WILL IT ACHIEVE?

We all have a right to clean air. You will have had a positive impact on people's health and well-being and reduced harmful emissions in your local area. Just as importantly, you will have brought your community together, changed people's perspectives and created more of a sense of pride in your area by making it cleaner and greener.

WALK TO SCHOOL

'We need to stop the fossil-fuel industry.'

HELENA GUALINGA

PHOTO © WOMEN'S EARTH AND CLIMATE ACTION NETWORK
INTERNATIONAL - KATHERINE QUAID

Author's note: Unlike the other stories, Helena's story comes from public interviews and articles instead of a direct interview.

Dividing her time when growing up between Sarayaku, in the Amazon rainforest, and Finland, 17-year-old Helena Gualinga lived in anxious anticipation of what she might find every time she returned from Finland to her family and community in the rainforest. Oil companies had been damaging the sacred territories of her people since before she was born. The threat weighed heavy. It always loomed in the back of her mind.

The Kichwa indigenous people of Sarayaku live deep in the Amazon rainforest on the edge of the Bobonaza River in Ecuador. The community can only be reached by plane or canoe. The Sarayaku elders have a prophecy: when all other groups have surrendered to outside forces, the sons and daughters of Sarayaku will lead the resistance, they will not back down, a beacon of light as bright as the beating sun at midday.

In 1996, the Ecuadorian government gave permission for an oil company to use Sarayaku community lands without consulting the Sarayaku people. In 2002, the year Helena was born, the company entered their lands with the support of the military to search for oil. They perpetrated acts of violence on members of the community and destroyed sacred areas. Helena's aunts and uncles fought back with the rest of their community. They wouldn't become another indigenous community destroyed and poisoned by companies extracting fossil fuels. They would be a beacon of light – they would resist.

When Helena was 10, Sarayaku's fight for justice moved publicly from the forest to the court room. Her community took their case against the government of Ecuador to the Inter-American Commission on Human Rights and they won. The government would now have to consult indigenous groups before allowing oil companies in.

Helena started joining protests with members of her family at a young age. As she grew up, it became clear the fight would be a long one and that these companies would continue to pose a threat to her community. She became more aware that these same companies were causing global heating and climate breakdown. Not only would they destroy her home, but they would destroy the planet too.

She couldn't let this happen. As an activist, she began to post on the internet and attend events. Indigenous groups are at the heart of the fight for a cleaner, greener and more just world and she would speak for them where she could. As an active member of the youth climate movement, she joined a panel at the latest UN climate conference. She spoke passionately about the need for indigenous people's voices to be heard and for the criminal behaviour of fossil-fuel companies and the governments that support them to stop.

In 2020, disappointed by the failure of the COP25 climate talks in Madrid, and the continued influence the fossil-fuel industry has over governments and other decision-makers, she launched a new initiative, 'Polluters Out', with other young climate activists. Along with scientists, indigenous people and grassroots groups across the world, these young change makers want to remove the influence of fossil-fuel companies, and secure stronger rights for indigenous groups who are on the front line of our fight for the planet.

Helena calls herself a 'daughter of the first uprising'. She embodies the Sarayaku prophecy.

HELENA'S MESSAGE TO YOU

I know that this is what I have to do. Give a voice to the people that have been silenced and the people that don't have a voice. We need to stop the fossil-fuel industry.

TIME TO DIVEST

HOW TO SET UP A DIVESTMENT CAMPAIGN AND STOP
FUNDING FOSSIL-FUEL COMPANIES

- -

WHY?

- Financial investment means putting money into
  something, like a business, in the same way that you
  would invest time, energy or effort. Divestment is the
  opposite. It is about taking money out, specifically out
  of fossil-fuel companies.

- To avoid devastating impacts on people and the planet,
  we need to keep 80% of the world's remaining fossil fuels
  where they belong, in the ground. To do that we need to
  stop the companies that are taking them out of the ground.

- Investing in fossil-fuel companies encourages them to
  continue extracting fossil fuels, which will continue the
  cycle of climate destruction. Divestment is a strategy for
  striking right at the heart of fossil-fuel companies.

Even if you can't divest yourself, by encouraging institutions
like faith groups, museums, theatres, universities or local
governments to divest their money away from fossil-fuel
companies, we can remove these funds and send a powerful
message to the companies that they need to change.

CAMPAIGN TIPS

- Check out 350.org's skill-up course, which will get you up
  to speed on divestment. The Fossil Free Network also has a
  whole range of useful resources and contacts for setting up
  a divestment campaign, with networks in many different
  countries that can be accessed through their central
  website.

- Approach other organizations campaigning on this issue
  and ask for help – in this case the Fossil Free Network,

Friends of the Earth and perhaps other groups similar to your target that have already successfully divested.

- Fossil Free UK has a helpful petition tool that you can use to collect signatures online.

- Identify reasons why ending fossil-fuel use is an urgent priority. Make sure you understand what divestment involves and be specific in the aim of your campaign about the timescale for divestment and reinvestment in renewable energy. For example, 'To convince group X to divest entirely from fossil fuels over the next five years'.

- Decide on 2–4 goals that will help you achieve your aim. For example:

  - Get group X to freeze any future investments in fossil fuels immediately.

  - Encourage group X to publish a signed statement committing to complete divestment in the next five years.

  - Persuade group X to end a sponsorship deal with a fossil-fuel company within the next year.

- Use the Tips for Talking About the Environmental Crisis (on page 161) when making your soft approach.

- Make sure you identify any public commitments that your target organization has made on the climate crisis before you approach them.

WHAT WILL IT ACHIEVE?

Convincing a group to divest is a formidable task and when you are successful it will be a significant achievement. You are contributing to one of the biggest movements for good in human history. While one organization divesting might seem like a small thing, your campaign could be one of thousands with similar goals, representing trillions of dollars. This sends a powerful message to fossil-fuel companies that people will no longer tolerate the harm they are doing to the planet and all life on it. It is time for them to change, and until they do, we will remove our support, stop financing their businesses and make it socially unacceptable to associate with them.

PESKY PESTICIDES

END THE USE OF DANGEROUS PESTICIDES THAT ARE
HARMFUL TO HUMANS AND WILDLIFE

WHAT ARE PESTICIDES?

Pesticides are chemical substances used to kill animals,
plants, fungi and bacteria that we consider to be pests – like
an insect that is damaging crops or weeds growing in a
garden lawn. There are hundreds of types of pesticide and
they are used everywhere – on farms, in gardens, parks and
on pavements and road verges.

WHY?

- The problem with pesticides is that they don't just harm
  the species they target – they poison wildlife, such as birds
  and insects. They harm those further up the food chain too,
  including humans!

- The World Health Organization estimates that every year
  pesticides kill hundreds of thousands of people around the
  globe directly through ingestion, and evidence links them
  to a number of serious illnesses.

- More and more pesticides are being used around the world,
  with a 24% increase in the UK between 2000 and 2016.

It is time to take a stand against these harmful chemicals that
are poisoning our Earth, our wildlife and our bodies. Here's how
you can help.

CAMPAIGN TIPS

- Look for signs that pesticides are being used in parks, on farms or along road verges. Ask around and politely check with your local council or farm whether they use them.

- Research the alternatives to pesticides, such as organic farming methods and natural pest management. There are plenty of pesticide-free methods for controlling pests in urban areas too; the Pesticide Action Network (PAN) has a good list of resources.

- Make your aim specific, for instance: 'To ban the use of pesticides in X park or in X borough to stop harmful impacts on insect pollinators, such as bees, and on humans.'

- The PAN has lots of helpful tools and guides. They even have a campaign to make your town pesticide-free!

- Once you are successful, use your new campaign skills and powers of persuasion elsewhere. Look at other areas in your region. Are there pesticides being used?

- Look at how you can avoid pesticides in your diet and buy food that will encourage pesticide-free food production (see Chapter 3).

WHAT WILL IT ACHIEVE?

The more energy and noise we create, the greater the chance that governments will take notice and ban the use of harmful pesticides, creating a healthier, safer place to live for people and wildlife.

ACTION 31   WIN IT, DON'T BIN IT

CAMPAIGN FOR MORE RECYCLING BINS IN YOUR AREA

--- --- --- --- --- --- --- --- --- --- --- --- --- --- --- ---

WHY?

- We create over 26 million tonnes of household waste each year in the UK, which is equivalent to the weight of 150,000 blue whales – many times more than are alive in our oceans today.

- In the UK less than 50% of our household waste is recycled even though around 80% of it could be.

- The energy used to make one aluminium drinks can from raw materials is the same as the amount it takes to recycle 20 aluminium drinks cans.

It makes financial and environmental sense to cut down on needless waste and recycle more of what we throw away. If we are committed, we can reduce the amount of energy and materials we use every minute of every day.

CAMPAIGN TIPS

- Identify who is responsible for the area where you would like bins installed – this will be your target.

- Conduct a clean-up in the area over a period of 1–2 weeks using Action 19 on page 110 and record the amount of litter you collect. Make sure you separate out any rubbish that can be recycled and record this too. This will provide evidence of the need for your bins.

- Develop a plan for how to get people using the bins.

- Design a competition that will engage other young people in recycling – perhaps you could have prizes or a reward after a set amount of recyclable material has been collected.

- Have an idea of who is going to empty the bins when they are full. Contact your local council about how to source the bins and about recycling collection and how often material is collected.

- When making your soft approach, you could offer to fundraise to help pay for the costs of the recycling bins (use page 198 in the 'Tips and Tricks' chapter for ideas).

- Monitor your success by conducting a series of clean-ups at the site over the course of the next month and compare the results to your original clean-ups.

- Change your competition after a few months to create a new incentive and keep it interesting.

- Come up with ways to educate people about recycling at your site. Perhaps you could create some information boards that explain why these bins were installed and by whom, and include a space where you can share up-to-date information on how much waste has been recycled at your site and the reduction in litter measured through your clean-ups.

WHAT WILL IT ACHIEVE?

The average person throws away up to seven times their body weight in waste every year. Recycling just one glass bottle will save enough energy to power a light bulb for four hours. So, if you install recycling bins in a place where there is a need, and get people using them, you could make a significant positive contribution. By tackling throw-away culture in this way you are simultaneously educating people about how to help the environment and having a direct impact on the amount of waste that is sent to landfill.

ACTION 32 SEA SENSE

CREATE A CAMPAIGN TO STOP LITTER ENTERING OUR OCEANS

WHY?

- Plastic waste kills up to a million seabirds each year, and 100% of marine turtles tested by scientists have been found to have plastic in their bodies.

- By 2050, the weight of plastic in the ocean could exceed the combined weight of all fish.

As an island nation we have a special responsibility to keep our coasts clean and our oceans clear, and with no one in the UK living more than 70 miles from the sea, we have a brilliant opportunity to do it.

CAMPAIGN TIPS

- You don't have to live near the sea to help protect it. Lots of waste flows into our oceans from rivers.

- Use Action 20 on page 116 to organize a river or beach clean. Record what you collect as this will be powerful evidence for your campaign case.

- One of the best solutions to the problem is to stop people littering in the first place, but you can also encourage people to buy plastic-free alternatives and get them involved in clean-ups too.

- Make sure to involve other young people in or outside of school in taking action with you. If regular beach or river clean-up days involving more young people are an outcome of your campaign, then it is a huge success.

- Use your campaign skills and experience to extend this approach to other areas or beaches locally.

WHAT WILL IT ACHIEVE?

There is so much we can do right on our doorstep to tackle the problem of ocean pollution. Whether it is stopping litter from flowing down our rivers to the sea or cleaning up our precious beaches, you are taking action to solve a global problem. Your actions will create waves of change in other people's understanding and behaviour and their sense of pride in the places where they live.

HANA'S STORY

'Don't lose hope. No matter how big or small, there is loads you can do.'
HANA SALIH

An article in *National Geographic* magazine about the climate crisis and extinction grabbed 13-year-old Hana Salih's attention. The polar bear in the photo next to the article seemed to be staring out at her. As she read, she felt more and more depressed and overwhelmed by the state of the world: habitat loss, climate breakdown, species extinction. What could she possibly do, living in the middle of Sheffield?

She decided that the one thing that she could do was make changes to her own behaviour. She swapped to a reusable water bottle, started reducing the amount of meat she ate and began to be careful about what food and clothing she bought and where it came from. Next, she wrote a letter to her head teacher and school catering company about single-use plastics and asked if they could stop using it. But Hana didn't get a response and she felt sad. It didn't seem like anyone else cared and she was afraid to stand out. How could she ever solve these massive problems alone?

Then the school strikes for climate began. She attended the first strike in Sheffield and felt empowered by so many people her age coming together. Hana was surprised to see that several other students from her school were there too. Maybe she was not as alone as she had thought. Together they decided to set up a group in school and they wrote to the head teacher and catering company about plastic packaging again. This time they did get a response and the school started reducing plastic use. Progress.

Hana saw that she could achieve so much more by joining others and having one united voice calling for change. Inspired, her group started recruiting more people to be involved in the strikes. Her school hadn't known the first strike was happening, but once they found out that more were scheduled, they sent a letter to all students advising them not to go. Most students ignored the letter and kept on attending.

After Hana had gone to her second strike, her parents decided it would be right for her to follow the school's policy, so that she could focus on her school work. She was really disappointed, but she didn't let it stop her taking action in other ways. It doesn't always have to be big gestures, she thought to herself. She joined the Youth Strike 4 Climate group in Sheffield and started to help organize the strikes instead.

Now she helps make them happen, even when she's not allowed to be there herself. The strikes wouldn't take place without Hana and the rest of the team. They help educate others, promote the strikes, source sound systems, decide on the best dates and plan march routes. Through her quiet actions Hana is enabling thousands of young people to come together and have a louder voice. What started out as a personal interest has become a big part of Hana's personality. Having just turned 15, she is now proud to call herself an environmentalist. She's learnt that there will always have to be compromise and to embrace being flexible. She is proud of what she has achieved. In just over a year, Hana went from discovering the fight for a better future to being on the front lines.

HANA'S MESSAGE TO YOU

It is hard when you see headlines that say by 2030 there could be no ice left. We shouldn't take this as we are doomed. We should make it an opportunity. We could have more ice. Don't get hung up on the negatives. Don't lose hope. No matter how big or small, there is loads you can do. It can be satisfying on a personal level, but also you will know you have done something for everyone on the planet.

MEAT ME HALFWAY

CONVINCE YOUR SCHOOL TO PROVIDE MORE MEAT-FREE
OPTIONS AND MEAT-FREE DAYS

- -

WHY?

- Reducing the amount of meat we eat is essential if we are
  to tackle the climate emergency and ecological crisis.

- Animal agriculture is responsible for similar levels of
  greenhouse gas emissions to transport and is a leading
  cause of habitat loss and species extinctions.

It is time to convince those around us that we can't go on
trashing the planet through the food we eat. This is a simple
thing we can all do to have a big, positive impact.

CAMPAIGN TIPS

- Over a week, work out how often your school canteen
  serves meat.

- Research a list of 8–10 environmental, health and cost
  benefits of meat-free days.

- Find out who decides on the school menus and where the
  food is sourced from. It is likely to be a combination of
  your head teacher, other senior teachers and your catering
  department, but there could be others.

- In some cases, an external company will be in charge of
  your school catering and that of a number of other schools.
  This is even better; it is a chance to change things in more
  than one school.

- Approach the decision-makers and ask if they would
  consider introducing meat-free days and sourcing high-
  quality, local, organic meat for the days meat is served.

- If your soft approach is unsuccessful, try getting support
  from the students with a petition and present this to

your school's management. If this doesn't work, then a boycott of the school canteen can be particularly effective at encouraging your key decision-makers to listen to your concerns.

- Investigate if it might be possible to grow food at your school using Action 13 on page 78 and get the school to use it in their school canteen or sell it to parents to fund other environmental projects at school.

WHAT WILL IT ACHIEVE?

If your school canteen served a cheeseburger every day for a school year and 500 students and teachers decided to eat one each day, they would be responsible for 237.5 tonnes CO_2e, the same amount of greenhouse gas emissions as cutting down almost half a hectare of rainforest. If students and staff swapped to a veggie burger, they would save 142.5 tonnes CO_2e. By encouraging everyone to go vegetarian on meat-free days, you can have a huge positive impact on the environment.

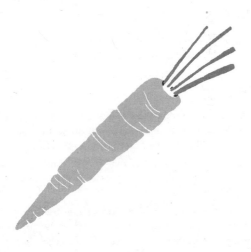

SUSTAINABLE SUPERMARKETS

SET UP A CAMPAIGN TO MAKE YOUR LOCAL SUPERMARKET MORE SUSTAINABLE AND ETHICAL

- -

WHY?

- Supermarkets have a huge amount of political and economic power within our global food system.

- In 2017, almost a third of all food sales around the world were made by the ten largest supermarket chains.

- There has been a huge growth in supermarket own-brand products, which account for over 40% of national food sales in the UK. Own-brand products can be sourced from around the world and are therefore less reliant on local producers or suppliers. There is also very little labelling on things like pesticide use.

Some supermarkets are making commitments to behave in a more responsible way, managing issues such as food waste and packaging and selling food that is produced more sustainably. It is time we held them to account and pushed them to do much better. We need a food system that works for the planet and changing how supermarkets are run is a big step towards this.

CAMPAIGN TIPS

- There are several online guides that rank how different supermarkets perform in terms of sustainability, such as the Good Shopping Guide and Ethical Consumer.

- Make sure you look online at your target supermarket's website to see what public commitments they have made on the environment, too.

- Explore what packaging your target supermarket is using for fruit and vegetables and whether they provide packaging-free refills for dry goods, such as cereals or pasta.

- Look at how clear their labelling is in the store. Is it easy to see which produce is organic and which options are more sustainable? Are there enough sustainable products to choose from? Are any of their own-brand products certified as organic or Fairtrade?

- Make a soft approach using information in the campaign guide and if it doesn't work, try out a petition, followed by a supermarket boycott and a protest outside to make it more impactful and raise awareness of your cause.

- The larger the boycott and protest, the more you hold and the longer they are, the more pressure you will put on the supermarket's management to discuss your proposals seriously. Use local and national press to gain attention.

- If you come up against problems convincing just one supermarket in a chain to change, then use your clever campaign skills and powers of persuasion to take your campaign national and contact the senior managers for the whole supermarket chain explaining the changes you think are necessary and why.

WHAT WILL IT ACHIEVE?

Supermarkets are big, powerful businesses – if you can create change here then the sky is the limit. You have sent a clear message to some of the largest players in our global food system, as well as to your local community, that your generation will demand higher standards and food that doesn't cost the earth.

YETUNDE'S STORY

'Speak about the issues that are troubling you. Spread your word. Don't hide in the shadows.'

YETUNDE KEHINDE

PHOTO © JADE OSAMWONYI

At 14 years old, Yetunde Kehinde left the city to visit the countryside for the first time for an environmental camp. She was excited and a little nervous. That first moment when she stepped out on to a wide expanse of sand and looked out to sea felt liberating. She wanted to run into the water. She found the camp inspiring and when she returned home, she was determined to build on this experience and speak up about the issues she cared about.

From the beginning, Yetunde decided she would just say things how she saw them and be honest about her own experiences. She was motivated by helping people to engage with local issues and make a difference in their communities. She believed that most people would not worry about big issues like climate breakdown until they saw how these problems would affect them and people they care about.

Yetunde's messages were clear and simple. She talked about the personal benefits nature provides, like clean air for us to breathe. She explained how environmental issues are also social issues – they can't be separated out. She showed how what we do today can have an impact on tomorrow.

People could hear her voice cutting through the noise and they listened to what she was saying. She was invited to feature in a film about taking action for the environment that the government was creating. She became an Ambassador for a youth social action initiative called the #IWill campaign. She even ended up hosting the launch event for their year of green action alongside the Minister for the Environment. Things didn't stop there: she recorded podcasts for Action for Conservation while suspended in a tree, became a judge at an event for their WildED school workshop programme and joined a handful of young people, including Esther, to launch the latest State of Nature report.

Sometimes Yetunde has found it hard to balance her school work, her weekend job and her environmental activism. When it came to deciding what degree to study at university and which career to pursue, she felt a lot of pressure from her community to become a doctor, accountant or banker. The trouble was, Yetunde was inspired by everything she had done for nature. She could see an exciting life spreading out before her and she knew that the next step was to get a degree in Geography. So, she ignored what everyone else said and applied to do just that. The University of Oxford has offered her a place, making her parents very proud.

YETUNDE'S MESSAGE TO YOU

Change is coming. Speak out! Speak about the issues that are troubling you. Spread your word. Don't hide in the shadows. Your word is powerful. A collective voice is louder than one voice, but even that one voice can speak a thousand things and reach so many places. I have always said what I believed and that is what is important. Do what you feel is important. I am looking forward to what we can achieve as young people together.

HOW TO SOURCE MATERIALS

For many of the actions in this book you may be able to scavenge materials for free. With a bit of looking around, you can often find things people no longer want at home, in school or in your local community. Remember, if you are taking something from a skip or something you think may no longer be wanted, always ask permission (see page 191).

If you can't find a free source of materials you can ask companies or local businesses whether they can help provide what you need for free. If you explain that it is for a good cause they might be able to help. As a last resort you can buy the things you need and fundraise to cover the costs (see page 198).

Below is a list of some of the things you might need for the actions in this book, along with advice about which options are most eco-friendly and how best to get your hands on them.

WOOD

Wood can be expensive and unsustainable if sourced from the wrong place (always look out for the Forest Stewardship Council [FSC] label to say wood you are buying is sustainably sourced and isn't leading to deforestation). You can also find wood that people are getting rid of and that you can use for free! It is always better to reuse. You can speak to local builders or timber merchants, explain your plans, and see if they can offer you any wood. Your school's Design and Technology department might have left-over wood that they can give you. Or just try asking family and friends if they have anything lying around. You might be able to scavenge wooden pallets from local shops, merchants or friends (ask permission!). If you intend to use some make sure it is safe first: reused wood can have nails in it, or be rotten. Incredible Edible have a helpful guide to making sure of this.

SEEDS

To source seeds in the UK at a low cost or for free, you can
contact organizations such as the RHS, Incredible Edible or
Kew Gardens. Wild flower seeds often come in ready-made
mixes and you can find out online which seeds are best to use.
Identify plants that are hardy (will survive well), need less
watering and that will be good for pollinating insects. It is
also better to use native wild flowers, plants that occur
naturally in your country; in the UK this includes plants like
yellow rattle, meadow buttercup and wild carrot. There is a
list of organizations that you can buy wild flower seeds from
on page 206.

TOOLS

For many practical actions you are likely to need some tools
and to know how to use them. You may be able to borrow tools
from your school, a parent or a friend's parent. It is much more
cost effective to borrow tools rather than buy them. Also,
remember you will need an adult's help for power tools, such
as drills. If you can't borrow what you need you may be able to
approach a local hardware shop and source them for free on a
temporary basis, or hire them.

PAPER AND PRINTING

Always buy or use recycled or sustainably sourced paper. Look for the FSC logo. You can buy environmentally friendly printer inks too. If you plan to print something at school or at home, find out what paper and ink is used and research whether more environmentally friendly options exist. If there are better options, make a proposal to your parent, guardian or head teacher explaining that you would like to help them source products that are better for the environment. If you need to use a professional printer for flyers or posters, then look for one with good environmental standards. Again, see if they will print your materials for free or at low cost first and if not, consider fundraising to cover printing costs (see page 198).

HOW TO IDENTIFY WHO OWNS LAND AND GET PERMISSION

- In some cases, you will need to identify the owner or person responsible for a particular space where you want to deliver an action. It is important to find the right person and ask for permission to use the space for your action. If it isn't immediately obvious who that is, for instance from signs or an online search, then ask around in your community. Contacting your local council is also a great place to start – you can easily find their contact details online. Your local council will also have specialists, such as tree officers, who may be able to give you advice, for example on planting trees.

- Before you make contact, you should have a clear plan for your action with research to back up your ideas. That way, when you get in touch, you can make a serious case for what you plan to do (see page 152 in the campaign guide for guidance on creating your case).

- Write them an email or letter (use Action 22 on page 127) stating your case and asking to arrange a meeting. Make sure to explain exactly what you need from them. It could be access to their land to conduct a survey or perhaps you plan to plant trees or install recycling bins.

- If you get a positive response, meet them (accompanied by a parent or guardian) to make the case in person and agree a timeline for gaining access to the land and taking action. Be prepared to negotiate at this stage and modify your plans if necessary.

HOW TO MEET WITH FIGURES OF AUTHORITY

- Make sure you have a clear, well-researched case for your project that covers all the main points.

- Know exactly what you want the person to do and have a plan for what you are going to say to them (see the campaign guide for tips, in particular the Tips for Talking About the Environmental Crisis on page 161).

- Practise saying your key points beforehand.

- Don't feel intimidated. The person has agreed to meet you and you have a good reason for being there. Remember, your ultimate purpose is to do good for the environment – you don't need to worry about one person's opinion, however important they may seem.

- If the conversation changes topic, bring it back to your key points and don't leave the meeting until you have got clear answers to your questions or a commitment from them that they will do something, even if it is a compromise.

HOW TO BUILD A TEAM

- Speak to your friends and family members about the problem. Explain the opportunity to create positive change and ask them to help you in making it happen. If your school already has an eco-team, you can ask members to join you in your project (see Action 21 on page 125 for advice on setting up a school eco-team).

- Set aside time to meet regularly and make sure you have an agenda. In the first meeting allow time for everyone to introduce themselves and have their say.

- You don't need everyone attending every meeting; it is more important to meet regularly to keep up momentum.

- Discuss each of your skills and what you can bring – it is good to have a mixture of skills. Think about what aspects of the project or campaign each team member is interested in: is it communications, writing, researching, hands-on activity?

- Use WhatsApp and email to communicate and store shared files using Google Drive or Dropbox.

- Building friendship and trust among members of the team will make you more successful.

WHERE YOU GET YOUR INFORMATION

The internet is incredibly useful, but be mindful that information on the internet can be created by anyone. Some sources are more reliable than others. If you are unfamiliar with your source, spend a little time researching the individuals or organizations involved. They may be funded by a particular company and have a particular agenda. This doesn't mean you can't use this information, but it is good to check your sources. Ask a parent, guardian or teacher to help you with this.

HOW TO CREATE A BUDGET FOR YOUR PROJECT

1. Start by making a list of everything you need for the project and find out how much each item will cost. Write down the cost of each item and add everything up to give you a total project 'Cost'. Next add up the money you have already spent or 'Amount Spent'. Put this in an expenditure table like the one below.

Note: you may be able to get some items for free, but it is best to create a worst-case scenario budget that includes all possible costs and then things can only get easier!

EXPENDITURE ITEM	COST	AMOUNT SPENT
10 PACKETS OF WILD FLOWER SEEDS	£25.00	£20.00
2 SPADES	£20.00	£0
3 BAGS OF PEAT-FREE COMPOST	£16.50	£5.50
TOTAL	£61.50	£25.50

2. Next, make a table listing all the sources for raising money. Add any money you have already raised from each source – your 'Amount Confirmed'. Add up the money you still hope to raise for your project from the different sources – your 'Amount to Raise'.

INCOME SOURCE	AMOUNT CONFIRMED	AMOUNT TO RAISE
BAKE SALE	£28.50	£0
SPONSORED WALK	£0	£20.00
FUNDRAISING COLLECTION	£5.00	£8.00
TOTAL	£33.50	£28.00

3. Put the two tables together into one table that you can update as you raise and spend money.

INCOME

INCOME SOURCE	AMOUNT CONFIRMED	AMOUNT TO RAISE
BAKE SALE	£28.50	£0
SPONSORED WALK	£0	£20.00
FUNDRAISING COLLECTION	£5.00	£8.00
TOTAL	£33.50	£28.00

EXPENDITURE

EXPENDITURE ITEM	COST	AMOUNT SPENT
10 PACKETS OF WILD FLOWER SEEDS	£25.00	£20.00
2 SPADES	£20.00	£0
3 BAGS OF PEAT-FREE COMPOST	£16.50	£5.50
TOTAL	£61.50	£25.50

4. Now you can add a row that shows how much you have spent compared with how much you have left to spend from the money you have raised. It is important to keep this up to date, so that you can keep on top of your finances.

INCOME

INCOME SOURCE	AMOUNT CONFIRMED	AMOUNT TO RAISE
BAKE SALE	£28.50	£0
SPONSORED WALK	£0	£20.00
FUNDRAISING COLLECTION	£5.00	£8.00
TOTAL	£33.50	£28.00

EXPENDITURE

EXPENDITURE ITEM	COST	AMOUNT SPENT
10 PACKETS OF WILD FLOWER SEEDS	£25.00	£20.00
2 SPADES	£20.00	£0
3 BAGS OF PEAT-FREE COMPOST	£16.50	£5.50
TOTAL	£61.50	£25.50
AMOUNT CONFIRMED INCOME – AMOUNT SPENT	£33.50 – £25.50 = £8.00	

HOW TO FUNDRAISE FOR A PROJECT

1. Use your budget to identify how much money you need to raise. Break the amount down; it is much better to be specific about what you are raising money for. You could even give examples of how certain amounts of money will be used. For example, £10 will pay for four packs of wild flower seeds, which will help to create three square metres of wild flower meadow.

2. Think about how you are going to raise the target amount. It is a good idea to use a mix of approaches. Here are a few ideas:

   - Host a bake sale.*

   - Get sponsored to walk, run or swim a certain distance.

   - Set up a video-game competition that people have to pay to enter.

   - Set up a film night or club at your school and sell tickets.

   - Create a stall selling upcycled items (see Action 16 on page 96).

   - Do a collection outside the school gates with permission from the head teacher.

   - Invite a speaker from an environmental charity to speak at your school and sell tickets to pupils and parents. This will work particularly well if the speaker's work relates to the cause or project you are raising money for.

   - Run a crowdfunding campaign online. It is important to create a video and use lots of eye-catching photos if you are going to fundraise online. It is also a good idea to make the fundraising window quite small, between two and four weeks. Make sure an adult is supervising this activity.

   - Use your imagination!

* Make sure you check with your school or local authority, if necessary, before holding a bake sale.

3. Always let people know what your target is and keep everyone up to date with your progress.

4. Advertise by creating posters, vlogs, posting online or speaking at assemblies. You want as many people as possible to know about your events and activities.

5. Once you reach your target be flexible. You can increase your target amount if you think that extra money will help.

6. Make sure to thank everyone who donated.

HOW TO SET UP A VOLUNTEER PROGRAMME

1. Write a one-page advert for the volunteering opportunity, including:

   - Summary of the project and the opportunity.

   - A clear explanation of why you want volunteers.

   - What skills will be required to become a volunteer.

   - What volunteers will get out of it, including experiences and any skills.

   - How often you need people and for what sort of time period.

   - What you would expect people to commit to as a minimum.

   - Information on how to apply – make this simple, like a short paragraph about themselves and why they'd like to volunteer.

   - Set a deadline for applications and give an email address or request applications are printed and given to a teacher.

2. Post the advert online on your school website and hand out and pin up flyers with the information around your school.

3. Assess the applications after the deadline and then make a decision on who you will take.

4. Speak to volunteers and ask them how much time they want to commit.

5. Create a rota with who is volunteering and when, and share this with everyone involved.

6. Send reminders before each shift with the date, time and location to each volunteer, and make sure there is always someone there to greet them and supervise them during the shift.

7. Find ways to thank volunteers. You could send regular messages updating everyone as your project progresses. If your project is creating or growing something, like upcycled furniture or fresh vegetables, then perhaps you can give them some for free as a reward.

8. Ask volunteers for regular feedback so that you can improve their experience of volunteering.

HOW TO CONTACT THE MEDIA

It is a great idea to get press coverage for your project as this will ensure more people find out about what you are doing. It can lead to further support and encourage other people to change their behaviour too. Here are some tips for getting in touch with journalists:

- Think about your story and why a journalist would want to cover it. What makes it exciting?

- Put together an email explaining your project in three sentences. Make sure you explain what you are doing, why you are doing it, who is involved, and when and where you are doing it. If you have one, attach a photo of the project to get them interested.

- Journalists like to cover events where there are photo opportunities, so think about something you can invite them to in relation to your project. Give them the date, time and location.

- Prepare the key points you want to make about your project in case they interview you or another team member.

- Whether or not a journalist attends, once your project or a particular part of your project, like an event, is complete, create a press release. A press release is intended to give journalists everything they need in order to write a story. There are plenty of templates for how to create one online. Your press release should be factual and say what happened. You should also include quotes from people involved in the project to make it interesting and include photos they can use.

USEFUL RESOURCES

There are many useful groups, organizations, societies and individuals with information and resources that can help you in your activities. Some of them are listed here. Go to their websites for more details.

BUSY SKIES

Guides for building insect hotels, bird and bat boxes
Royal Society for the Protection of Birds (RSPB)
The Wildlife Trusts

HOW TO BECOME A CITIZEN SCIENTIST

iRecord app or iNaturalist app can be used to record any species you identify while surveying.
Woodland Trust: Nature's Calendar (to help understand impacts of the climate crisis on wildlife)

HEDGEROW SURVEYS FOR PLANTS AND INSECTS

Open Air Laboratories (OPAL) network

TREE SURVEYS

OPAL network: Tree health survey
Woodland Trust: Ancient tree hunt; Tree ID app

WILD FLOWER SURVEYS

Plantlife

INSECT SURVEYS

OPAL network: Insects; pollinating insects; water insects
UK Centre for Ecology & Hydrology (CEH): Pollinating insects
Big Butterfly Count

AMPHIBIAN AND REPTILE SURVEYS

Froglife: Dragon Finder app

MAMMAL SURVEYS

People's Trust for Endangered Species (PTES)

National Biodiversity Network
The Mammal Society
Bat Conservation Trust (BCT)

BIRD SURVEYS
British Trust for Ornithology (BTO): Bird Track
RSPB: Garden Birdwatch
Cornell Lab of Ornithology: eBird app

EARTHWORM SURVEYS
Natural History Museum, London
OPAL network: Soil quality and earthworm survey

AIR QUALITY SURVEY
OPAL network

FUN IN THE FIELD
Field Studies Council (FSC)
RSPB
The Wildlife Trusts

THE ORIGINAL SKYSCRAPERS

PLANNING WHERE TO PLANT
Woodland Trust: Woodland Trust Planting Planning Tool
Forest Research: Urban Tree Manual

CHOOSING A TREE TO PLANT
Forest Research
Royal Horticultural Society (RHS)
Woodland Trust

SOURCING FREE TREES
Woodland Trust

PLANT FOR POLLINATORS

Landlife Wildflowers

Sarah Raven

RHS

RSPB

Kew Gardens

WALK ON THE WILD SIDE

Kaul of the Wild

Biological Records Centre (BRC)

HIGHWAYS FOR HEDGEHOGS

Hedgehog Street: pictures of different holes; pledge to create a hedgehog hole; add the location of your hole or any hedgehog sightings to their map; see whether hedgehogs have been seen in your area.

The British Hedgehog Preservation Society: recycled plastic sign for your hedgehog hole.

EAT GREEN

National Health Service (NHS): The Vegetarian Diet; The Vegan Diet

World Wide Fund for Nature (WWF): Livewell report

The Vegan Society

GROW YOUR OWN FOOD

GUIDES FOR PLANTING AND HARVESTING

Incredible Edible Network: Crop planner; Extending the growing season; Fruit and vegetables in season

SEED TRAYS

Incredible Edible Network

COLLECTING AND GROWING SEEDS

Incredible Edible Network: Growing from seed; Seed saving

FOOD FOR THOUGHT

Sustain: Sustainable food

Ethical Consumer: Food and drink

Marine Conservation Society: *Good Fish Guide*

CLEAN GREEN

Keep Britain Tidy

RIPPLE EFFECT

The Rivers Trust

Canal & River Trust

UK Rivers Network

Thames21

Surfers Against Sewage

National Trust

SPEAK TRUTH TO THOSE IN POWER

UK Parliament

FIND A PROTEST

UK Student Climate Network

FIND YOUR PLACE

Young Trustees Movement

PLANE DRAIN

Flight Free campaign

ENOUGH ENGINES

National Atmospheric Emissions Inventory: UK Emissions Map

ClientEarth

OTHER ORGANIZATIONS

Friends of the Earth: Clean Air Campaign

Global Action Plan: Clean Air Day

British Lung Foundation: Campaign for Cleaner Air

Campaign for Better Transport

Transition Network

TIME TO DIVEST

Fossil Free (including a UK petition tool)

350.org: Skill-up course

PESKY PESTICIDES

Look out for articles on pesticides in the press. You can also find information on pesticides from the following:

Friends of the Earth

World Health Organization

State of Nature report 2019

Change.org

Pesticide Action Network (PAN)

SUSTAINABLE SUPERMARKETS

The Good Shopping Guide

Ethical Consumer

TIPS AND TRICKS

Incredible Edible Network: guide to ensure pallets are safe

Gov.uk website: how to find and contact your local council

GLOSSARY

ACCOUNTABLE
To be responsible for what you do and to be able to give good reasons for it.

BAT DETECTOR
A device used to detect the presence of bats and identify different bat species by converting their echolocation calls into audio frequencies that we can hear.

BIODEGRADE
The process of bacteria or other living organisms breaking down a substance or object.

BIRDWATCHING HIDE
A birdwatching hide or bird hide is a small room, cabin or other structure that allows you to remain hidden while watching birds or other animals.

BOYCOTT
A deliberate act of protest where you stop using, buying, or dealing with a person, organization or country on social, political or environmental grounds.

CIRCULAR ECONOMY
An economic system based on the principle of eliminating waste and pollution and instead keeping products and materials in continual use.

CITIZEN SCIENTIST
A member of the public who collects and analyses data, often to contribute to large-scale research projects involving professional scientists.

CLIMATE BREAKDOWN
Serious, harmful changes to the world's climate, including extreme weather events, brought about by global heating.

CLIMATE CRISIS AND CLIMATE EMERGENCY

Terms used to describe global heating and climate breakdown and the threat they pose to the planet.

CONSTITUENCY

An area whose voters elect a representative or official, like a politician.

CROP

A plant like a grain, fruit or vegetable that is typically, but not always, grown for food.

ECOLOGICAL CRISIS

Widespread species extinctions and declines caused by rapid environmental changes. The current ecological crisis is being brought about by human activities such as logging, farming and urban development, as well as climate breakdown.

ECOSYSTEM

A community of biological organisms that interact with each other and the physical environment where they live.

ENVIRONMENTAL CRISIS

A more general term to describe the climate crisis and the ecological crisis together.

EXTINCTION

The loss of a species. Usually considered to be the moment the last individual of that species dies.

FOSSIL FUELS

Naturally occurring non-renewable fuels such as petroleum, coal or gas that release large quantities of carbon dioxide when burnt for energy. Human use of fossil fuels is the leading cause of global heating and climate breakdown.

GLOBAL HEATING

The ongoing rise of the average temperature of the Earth's atmosphere, also known as global warming.

GRASSROOTS CAMPAIGN

A campaign led by people from a place or community who take collective action at a local level to bring about change at a local, regional, national or international scale.

HABITAT

The natural home of animals, plants and other organisms.

HEDGEROW

A line of different species of tree and bush growing close together, usually along the boundary of a field, road, woodland, park or other open area.

LEGACY

Something that you leave behind, as part of your history.

LIVELIHOOD

How someone earns money to pay for food, shelter and other necessities.

MICROPLASTIC

Extremely small pieces of plastic that are released into the environment or created when larger plastic items break down over time.

NATIVE SPECIES

A species that occurs naturally and thrives in a particular place or ecosystem. This does not typically include species that have been introduced to new areas that they would not otherwise have existed in.

PLASTIC MICROFIBRES

A type of microplastic. These small thread-like fibres come from synthetic fabrics like polyester.

POLLINATE/POLLINATING

To take pollen from one plant or a part of a plant to another so that new seeds can be produced. For example, bees carry pollen from one flower to another, so they are pollinating insects. Pollination is an important part of plant reproduction.

PUBLIC LIABILITY INSURANCE

Insurance that covers the costs of legal claims made by members of the public for incidents that occur in connection with particular activities. For example, the cost of compensation for someone who suffers an injury while picking up litter as part of an organized clean-up.

RECYCLING

A process where waste materials are converted into materials that can be reused.

REPURPOSING

The action of adapting an object for a different use.

ROAD VERGE

The strip of plants, grass and sometimes trees that runs along the side of a road.

SOURCE

To find or get hold of something like information or materials.

SPECIES

A group of living organisms that are similar and capable of interbreeding and producing offspring.

TOKENISM

The process of making a symbolic, rather than a meaningful, effort to be inclusive of an individual or group. For example, officially and publicly appointing a young person as a decision-maker and then not listening to them when decisions actually need to be made.

UPCYCLING

The activity of turning old objects such as furniture or clothing into a new object.

REFERENCES

ACTION 1

www.rspb.org.uk/about-the-rspb/about-us/media-centre/press-releases/let-nature-sing-wales

www.birdlife.org/sites/default/files/attachments/BL_ReportENG_V11_spreads.pdf

www.bto.org/press-releases/where-are-all-turtle-doves-and-partridges

ACTION 2

www.un.org/sustainabledevelopment/blog/2019/05/nature-decline-unprecedented-report

ACTION 3

www.theguardian.com/education/2019/jul/21/education-school-trips-outings-teaching-pupils-budget-cuts

ACTION 4

www.climatefocus.com/sites/default/files/2019NYDF_ES.pdf

www.cityoftrees.org.uk/

www.manchester.gov.uk/download/downloads/id/25574/manchester_tree_action_plan.pdf

www.forestresearch.gov.uk/tools-and-resources/statistics/statistics-by-topic/woodland-statistics/

www.treesforcities.org/stories/trees-in-our-cities-10-reasons-we-need-to-plant-more

www.usda.gov/media/blog/2015/03/17/power-one-tree-very-air-we-breathe

www.co2meter.com/blogs/news/could-global-co2-levels-be-reduced-by-planting-trees

ACTION 5

www.sciencedirect.com/science/article/pii/S0006320718313636

www.bumblebeeconservation.org/wp-content/uploads/2017/08/
BBCT_Land_Factsheet_2_Managing_wildflower_meadows.pdf

www.plantlife.org.uk/uk/about-us/news/devastation-of-
meadows-endangers-flower-favourites-like-wild-strawberry-
ragged-robin-and-harebell

ACTION 6

wwf.panda.org/our_work/wildlife/problems/habitat_loss_
degradation/

ACTION 7

www.london.gov.uk/what-we-do/environment/parks-green-
spaces-and-biodiversity/biodiversity

ACTION 8

www.hedgehogstreet.org/about-our-hedgehog-street-campaign/
stateof/

ACTION 10

uk-air.defra.gov.uk/air-pollution/causes

Berners-Lee, Mike, *How Bad are Bananas?* Profile Books, 2010

www.theguardian.com/environment/ng-interactive/2019/
jul/19/carbon-calculator-how-taking-one-flight-emits-as-much-
as-many-people-do-in-a-year

ACTION 11

www.ipcc.ch/site/assets/uploads/2018/02/ipcc_wg3_ar5_
chapter8.pdf

assets.publishing.service.gov.uk/government/uploads/system/
uploads/attachment_data/file/862887/2018_Final_greenhouse_
gas_emissions_statistical_release.pdf

www.who.int/mediacentre/news/releases/2014/air-pollution/en/

Berners-Lee, Mike, *How Bad are Bananas?* Profile Books, 2010

ACTION 12

www.worldwildlife.org/pages/why-wwf-cares-about-meat-poultry-dairy-and-seafood

www.fao.org/3/a0701e/a0701e.pdf

wwf.panda.org/our_work/wildlife/problems/habitat_loss_degradation/

www.sciencedirect.com/science/article/abs/pii/S0308521X1000096X?via%3Dihub

wwf.panda.org/knowledge_hub/all_publications/living_planet_report_2018/

assets.wwf.org.uk/downloads/livewell_report_jan11.pdf

www.nature.com/articles/s41586-018-0594-0.epdf

science.sciencemag.org/content/314/5800/787.abstract

www.pnas.org/content/113/18/5125

www.pnas.org/content/113/18/4895

Berners-Lee, Mike, *How Bad are Bananas?* Profile Books, 2010

ACTION 13

www.gov.uk/government/publications/food-statistics-pocketbook-2017/food-statistics-in-your-pocket-2017-global-and-uk-supply

ACTION 14

wwf.panda.org/our_work/food/?

www.who.int/news-room/detail/15-07-2019-world-hunger-is-still-not-going-down-after-three-years-and-obesity-is-still-growing-un-report

www.fao.org/food-loss-and-food-waste/en/

www.un.org/development/desa/en/news/population/world-population-prospects-2019.html

ACTION 15

www.ellenmacarthurfoundation.org/publications/a-new-textiles-economy-redesigning-fashions-future

www.worldwildlife.org/stories/the-impact-of-a-cotton-t-shirt

www.plymouth.ac.uk/news/washing-clothes-releases-thousands-of-microplastic-particles-into-environment-study-shows

www.sciencedirect.com/science/article/abs/pii/S2468584417300119

ACTION 16

www.overshootday.org/newsroom/press-release-june-2020-english/

ACTION 17

www.unenvironment.org/interactive/beat-plastic-pollution/

www.iucn.org/resources/issues-briefs/marine-plastics

plasticoceans.org/the-facts/

ACTION 18

www.unenvironment.org/interactive/beat-plastic-pollution/

www.wwf.org.au/news/blogs/the-lifecycle-of-plastics

www.postconsumers.com/2011/10/31/how-long-does-it-take-a-plastic-bottle-to-biodegrade/

www.wwf.org.au/news/blogs/how-many-birds-die-from-plastic-pollution

www.wwf.org.uk/updates/holiday-plastic-choking-our-oceans

www.ellenmacarthurfoundation.org/assets/downloads/EllenMacArthurFoundation_TheNewPlasticsEconomy_Pages.pdf

Berners-Lee, Mike, *How Bad are Bananas?* Profile Books, 2010

ACTION 19

www.keepbritaintidy.org/faqs/advice/litter-and-law

ACTION 20

www.bbc.co.uk/news/uk-england-49131405

www.theriverstrust.org/key-issues/water-quality/

www.nationalgeographic.com/environment/habitats/
freshwater-threats/

www.sas.org.uk/our-work/plastic-pollution/plastic-pollution-
facts-figures/

www.iucn.org/resources/issues-briefs/marine-plastics

www.cia.gov/library/publications/resources/the-world-factbook/
fields/282.html

ACTION 27

Berners-Lee, Mike, *How Bad are Bananas?* Profile Books, 2010

www.eci.ox.ac.uk/research/energy/downloads/jardine09-
carboninflights.pdf

www.bbc.com/future/article/20200218-climate-change-how-to-
cut-your-carbon-emissions-when-flying

www.gov.uk/government/publications/greenhouse-gas-
reporting-conversion-factors-2019

www.bbc.co.uk/news/science-environment-49349566

www.wwf.org.uk/sites/default/files/2017-09/WWF_Livewell_
Plates_Summary_Report_Sept2017_Web.pdf

ACTION 28

unearthed.greenpeace.org/2017/04/04/air-pollution-nurseries/

www.kcl.ac.uk/news/uk-air-pollution-could-cause-36000-deaths-
a-year

www.gov.uk/government/news/public-health-england-
publishes-air-pollution-evidence-review

www.who.int/mediacentre/news/releases/2014/air-pollution/en/

Helena's story

latinamericareports.com/helena-gualinga-voice-indigenous-communities-fight-climate-change/4192/

globalshakers.com/world-shakers/helena-gualinga/

2020.energydialogue.berlin/person/helena-gualinga/

www.wbur.org/hereandnow/2019/12/13/helena-gualinga-climate-change-activist

www.insider.com/greta-thunberg-activists-climate-change-who-are-they-2019-9#helena-gualinga-17-is-from-the-ecuadorian-amazon-and-said-shes-been-fighting-for-climate-issues-my-entire-life-2

sacredland.org/sarayaku-ecuador/

amazonwatch.org/work/sarayaku

amazonwatch.org/news/2018/0719-visionary-living-forest-proposal-to-be-launched-by-kichwa-people-of-sarayaku

ACTION 29

350.org/why-we-need-to-keep-80-percent-of-fossil-fuels-in-the-ground/

ACTION 30

www.sciencedirect.com/science/article/pii/S0041008X13000549

www.pan-uk.org/health-effects-of-pesticides/

www.who.int/ipcs/poisons/en/

friendsoftheearth.uk/nature/why-were-overusing-pesticides-uk-farmers-view

ACTION 31

assets.publishing.service.gov.uk/government/uploads/system/uploads/attachment_data/file/874265/UK_Statistics_on_Waste_statistical_notice_March_2020_accessible_FINAL_rev_v0.5.pdf

iwc.int/status

www.cardiff.gov.uk/ENG/resident/Rubbish-and-recycling/Take-it-to-the-tip/Other-ways-to-recycle-and-reuse/Pages/Other-ways-to-recycle-and-reuse.aspx

alupro.org.uk/consumers/why-is-recycling-aluminium-so-important/

www.recyclingbins.co.uk/recycling-facts/

friendsoftheearth.uk/natural-resources/7-benefits-recycling

ACTION 32

news.bbc.co.uk/1/hi/england/derbyshire/3090539.stm

sustainabledevelopment.un.org/content/documents/Ocean_Factsheet_Pollution.pdf

onlinelibrary.wiley.com/doi/10.1111/gcb.14519

www.ellenmacarthurfoundation.org/assets/downloads/EllenMacArthurFoundation_TheNewPlasticsEconomy_Pages.pdf

ACTION 33

www.fao.org/news/story/en/item/197623/icode/

www.iea.org/reports/tracking-transport-2019

www.wri.org/blog/2019/10/everything-you-need-know-about-fastest-growing-source-global-emissions-transport

www.ipcc.ch/site/assets/uploads/2018/02/ipcc_wg3_ar5_chapter8.pdf

ACTION 34

www.ipes-food.org/_img/upload/files/Concentration_FullReport.pdf

pdfs.semanticscholar.org/a320/23f679ee62e372ab8b1cc1c19d8a3ac0ee1f.pdf

www.prnewswire.com/news-releases/global--regional-food--grocery-retailing-2017-2022-market-size-forecasts-trends-and-competitive-landscape-300869494.html#

ACKNOWLEDGEMENTS

Thank you first and foremost to the incredible young people who feature in this book, those I have worked with through Action for Conservation and the many more around the world who are fighting for a better future. You are hopeful, indefatigable and a constant source of inspiration to us all.

I have a great deal of admiration and gratitude for the trustees and team at Action for Conservation, both past and present. I would not be in a position to write this book without your considerable commitment, friendship and support. Thank you, David Macdonald, for your leadership; Aoife Bennett, Helen Ghosh and John Fanshawe, for your advice and vision; Princess-Joy Emeanuwa, Serena Murdoch, Helen Bourne and Katarina Lundrigan, for your ideas and for keeping us grounded; Sam Piranty, for your brotherly love and the occasional prod in the right direction; Alex Mills, for your sage advice, your steady head and your unfailing friendship; Kate Huggett, for being there at the beginning; Laura Kravac, for making the charity what it is today and for reading and shaping the book; Hannah Ryan-Leah, for your dedication to our work, your keen eye and for your experienced and helpful suggestions for the book; Zunaira Malik, for your hard work, humour and for reading and commenting on the book; Emma Schofield, for all that you do to pioneer our work in the North West; Vicky Trigle, for your dedication and vital contributions to the charity's success, and Sophie Jones – it has been wonderful to welcome you to the team. Forrest Hogg, I am grateful for over a decade of kinship and deep friendship, and I feel privileged that we now have an opportunity to work together on a ground-breaking and exciting project. Finally, a special thank you to the inspiring Robert Macfarlane, for your mentorship, friendship and encouragement, for reminding me that stories change the world too and for writing a beautiful foreword to this book.

The hills and holloways of West Dorset, which weave their way round Bridport and down to the sea, have nurtured my strong roots and sense of place. Swimming out to sea to gaze back up at Golden Cap makes me feel alive and at home. To those who have been a part of my wild education and inspired, supported and guided me along the way, I am so grateful.

Thanks to all those at the Sir John Colfox Academy and
Beaminster School. Thank you, Will Allen, for your humour, for
always coming along for the ride and for keeping me in check.
Thank you, Sophie Perkins, for gently and wisely turfing us
out, rain or shine. Harry Owen, I am forever grateful for your
unswerving and loyal friendship. The thousands of hours of
play and adventure have shaped who we are, and I wouldn't
be here without you. Nick Hill, you taught me the art of
hedge-laying, and your steady presence and easy laughter
are so very grounding. Kate Guinness, thank you for your
warmth and many, many kindnesses, and Julia Schönbrunn,
for your encouragement and infectious spirit. Thanks to John
Zablocki, Francesca Fernandez, Matt Davey, Sam Phillips,
Gemma Taylor, Guy Western and the rest of the BCM crew,
too many to name and an influence on me too great to explain.
Vina, Gavin and Josh Hogg, I am incredibly grateful for
your friendship, generosity of spirit, energy and hospitality.
Dan Isles, it is always a pleasure to break bread, and John
Wiltshire, thank you for the rich and thoughtful conversation.
For shaping who I am, thanks are also due to: Will Baldwin-
Cantello, Chris, Jo, Jessie, Connie and Poppy Booth, Debbie
Chambers, Coco, Lydia Cole, Jim Dixon, Will Everitt, Dan
Gouly, Ellie Griffies Weld, Amy Hale, Britt Harrison, Curt
Hayward, Henry Hoskins, Alice Humphries, Jesse, Tilly and
Nic Jeune, Aisla Jones, Libby Jones, Emma Keller, Dan Leak,
Anna Ledgard, Lily Martin, Max, Freddie and Molly Owen,
Julia Petrenko, Hal Rhoades, Morven Robertson and Ben Vardy.

To all those in Arevalillo de Cega, and the *Rebeldes* in
particular, thank you for teaching me the true meaning of
community and for infusing my summers with magic below
vast blue Castilian skies. Whether gazing at shooting stars
from the *deposito* while wild boar root in the sunflower fields
below, or watching vultures soar above the beautiful Sierra de
Guadarrama, I feel a depth of connection difficult to describe.

Thank you to all the inspiring teachers and volunteers who
have given up their time to turn Action for Conservation into
what it is today – we owe you a great debt. The work that
we do is impossible without the incredible commitment and
generosity of our supporters and friends – thank you all for
believing in our approach.

I am forever grateful to Euan Thorneycroft at A. M. Heath; your trust and guidance has been invaluable. The team at Penguin have been incredible throughout the process of working with me to create this book. Thank you, Jamie Coleman, for first reaching out. Asmaa Isse, your hard work and creative input have brought this book to life and your optimistic schedule has kept me moving. It has been a pleasure to work with you. Thank you to the designers; Anita Mangan, your illustrations have made the book sing, and Emily Smyth, your cover design is wonderfully arresting. Thank you also to Holly Harris, Shreeta Shah, Julia Bruce, Felicity Trotman and Petra Bryce.

My family have given me strength and encouraged me. My mother, Alexandra van Hensbergen, gave me a love of nature in childhood, generously imparted her values, taught me to be an environmentalist and inspired me to start a charity. My father, Gijs van Hensbergen, has filled my life with stories, curiosity and laughter, taught me to be daring, and has relentlessly championed my work. Thank you for reading the book and for your helpful suggestions. My sister Rosa van Hensbergen and her husband, Ryan Pepin, are full of joy, humour and intelligence, and I love them dearly. A particular thank you to my sister Hester van Hensbergen for the formidable deftness and clarity of her edits. What a bright star you are. To my wife's family, who are now very much my own, Frances, François, Louise and Sebastien de Menthon, and Alex Pope, thank you for your great kindness, abundant love, and continuous support and encouragement. Thanks to my uncle Berty for inspiring me to study Zoology. I am grateful to my grandmother, Estelle Coulter, and my late grandfather, John Coulter, who, as well as my late oma and opa, Ans and Piet van Hensbergen, have given me a sense of adventure and of what it means to work hard. To the wider Coulter and van Hensbergen tribes, I thank you all with love.

Finally, to my wife, Sophie, you have been steadfast and none of this would be possible without your kind, loving support, your companionship and your indomitable spirit. Just like you, your comments on the manuscript came late, but were worth the wait. In December you brought our beautiful boy, Ludo, into the world in the midst of me writing the book. This little bundle of hope and joy spurred me on through the tiredness and winter darkness into the warmth of spring.

ABOUT ACTION FOR CONSERVATION

A proportion of the royalties from each copy of *How You Can Save the Planet* will be donated to Action for Conservation, a charity founded by Hendrikus van Hensbergen. The charity works to inspire and empower the next generation of environmental change makers, across the UK, many of whom are featured in this book, through workshops in schools, residential camps, an Ambassador scheme and an online action programme. In 2019 it launched the Penpont Project in Wales, the world's largest youth-led nature restoration initiative. Young people from Wales and across the UK are working with farmers and landowners to regenerate a site at Penpont Estate in the Brecon Beacons National Park and create a model that will inspire hope and action for generations to come. The charity welcomes all young people aged 12–18 on to their programmes – join them.

OTHER ORGANIZATIONS

A selection of other organizations and networks not already mentioned, both large and small, in the UK and internationally, that work with or for young people: Amazon Watch, BirdLife International, Black2Nature, Blue Marine Foundation, Children & Nature Network, Citizen Zoo, City to Sea, Conservation Optimism, The Conservation Volunteers, Country Trust, Durrell Wildlife Conservation Trust, Earth Guardians, Earthwatch Institute, Eco Schools, Elephant Family, Ellen MacArthur Foundation, EUROPARC Foundation, Fauna & Flora International, Focus on Nature, Forest Peoples Programme, Forum for the Future, Fridays For Future, Global Justice Now, Global Witness, Greenpeace, Green Schools Project, Groundwork, Hubbub, Indigenous Environmental Network, Islamic Relief, Jane Goodall's Roots & Shoots, John Muir Trust, May Project Gardens, National Park City Foundation, The Nature Conservancy, Possible, Semble, Students Organising for Sustainability UK, Sunrise Movement, Synchronicity Earth, Teach the Future, Trees for Cities, UK Youth Climate Coalition, Underhill Wood Nature Reserve, Vía Campesina, Voyage Youth, Whitley Fund for Nature, Wilderness Foundation UK, Wilderness Foundation Africa, Wildlife Conservation Research Unit, Wildlife and Countryside Link, Wildlife Conservation Society, Wildscreen, Women's Earth and Climate Action Network International, Youth for Our Planet and Zoological Society of London.

NOTES

NOTES